Cats are
SMARTER than JACK

89 amazing true cat stories

Connecting animal lovers and helping animals worldwide

The publisher
Smarter than Jack Limited (a subsidiary of Avocado Press Limited)
Australia: PO Box 170, Ferntree Gully, Victoria, 3156
Canada: PO Box 819, Tottenham, Ontario, L0G 1W0
New Zealand: PO Box 27003, Wellington
www.smarterthanjack.com

The creators
SMARTER than JACK series concept and creation: Jenny Campbell
Compiler and typesetting: Lisa Richardson
Administration: Anthea Kirk
Cover design: DNA Design, Simon Cosgrove and Lisa Richardson
Cover photograph: © Rachael Hale Photography (NZ) Ltd 2004. All rights reserved.
Rachael Hale is a registered trademark of Rachael Hale Photography Limited.
Illustrations: Martin Wilkinson
Story typing and editing: Patricia Reesby
Story selection: Jenny Campbell, Lisa Richardson, Lydia Crysell and others
Proofreading: Vicki Andrews (Animal Welfare in Print)
North American office: Eric Adriaans

The book trade distributors
Australia: Bookwise International
Canada: Publishers Group Canada
New Zealand: Addenda Publishing
United Kingdom: Airlift Book Company
United States: Publishers Group West

The participating animal welfare charities
The participation of the wonderful team at Cats Protection is gratefully acknowledged. This book can be purchased through Cats Protection, and through a number of other participating animal welfare charities. Please see the list on pages 146-148.

In the United Kingdom £3.00 from every sale made through Cats Protection and 10p from every bookshop sale of this book will be donated to Cats Protection. Cats Protection was not responsible for the production, design or distribution of this book.

The legal details
First published 2005
ISBN 0-9582571-6-7
SMARTER than JACK is a trademark of Avocado Press Limited
Copyright © 2005 Avocado Press Limited

Contents

Responsible animal care iv

Creating your SMARTER than JACK. v

Connecting animal lovers worldwide. vi

The enchanting cover photo vii

The delightful illustrations. vii

Foreword viii

1 Smart cats lend a paw 1

2 Smart cats take control 9

3 Smart cats take care of others 25

4 Smart cats find solutions and learn fast 43

Your say 57

5 Smart cats have fun and outwit others 61

6 Smart cats make us wonder 77

7 Smart cats prevent disasters 93

8 Smart cats take possession 107

9 Smart cats touch our hearts 125

The SMARTER than JACK story 139

Submit a story for our books. 141

Receive a free SMARTER than JACK gift pack. 143

Get more wonderful stories 145

Responsible animal care

The stories in this book have been carefully reviewed to ensure that they do not promote the mistreatment of animals in any way.

It is important to note, however, that animal care practices can vary substantially from country to country, and often depend on factors such as climate, population density, predators, disease control, local by-laws and social norms. Animal care practices can also change considerably over time; in some instances, practices considered perfectly acceptable many years ago are now considered unacceptable.

Therefore, some of the stories in this book may involve animals in situations that are not normally acceptable in your community. We strongly advise that you consult with your local animal welfare charity if you are in any way unsure about the best way to care for animals in your community.

You may also find, when reading these stories, that you can learn from other people's (often unfortunate) mistakes. We also advise that you take care to ensure your pet does not eat poisonous plants or other dangerous substances, and do not give any animal alcohol. In some rather extreme cases, you may even need to monitor what television channels your pet watches!

Creating your SMARTER than JACK

Cats are SMARTER than JACK is a heart-warming book of tales about truly smart cats. This is the first edition in the SMARTER than JACK series that is dedicated solely to cats.

Many talented and generous people have had a hand in the creation of this book. This includes everyone who submitted a story, and especially those who had a story selected as this provided the content for this inspiring book. The people who gave us constructive feedback on earlier books and cover design, and those who participated in our research, helped us make this book even better.

The team at Cats Protection assisted us greatly and were wonderful to work with. Profit from sales of this book in the United Kingdom will help Cats Protection, and profit from sales of this book in other countries will help many other animal welfare charities, in their admirable quest to improve animal welfare.

Steve Leonard wrote the moving foreword, Lisa Richardson compiled the stories, did the typesetting and helped with the cover design, Rachael Hale Photography provided the beautiful cover photograph, Pat Reesby typed and edited stories, Anthea Kirk helped coordinate all the entries, Vicki Andrews did the proofreading, Martin Wilkinson drew the lovely illustrations, and many others helped with the enormous task of selecting and typing the stories.

Thanks to bookstores for making this book widely available to our readers, and thanks to readers for purchasing this book and for enjoying it and for giving it to others as gifts.

Lastly, I cannot forget my endearing companion Ford the cat. Ford is now 12 years old and has been by my side all the way through the inspiring SMARTER than JACK journey.

We hope you enjoy **Cats are SMARTER than JACK** – and we hope that many animals and people benefit from it.

Jenny Campbell
Creator of SMARTER than JACK

Connecting animal lovers worldwide

Our readers and story contributors love to share their experiences and adventures with other like-minded people. So to help them along we've added a few new features to our books.

You can now write direct to many of the contributors about your experiences with the animals in your life. Some contributors have included their contact details with their story. If an email address is given and you don't have access to the internet, just write a letter and send it via us and we'll be happy to send it on.

We also welcome your letters for our 'Your say' section. These could be about animals in your life or about people who are out there making a difference.

Do you have an unusual question that other readers may be able to help answer? Some readers have posed a number of interesting questions, scattered throughout this book. Can you answer them?

Do you like to write to friends and family by mail? In the back of this book we've included some special SMARTER than JACK story postcards. Why not keep in touch and spread the smart animal word at the same time.

Since 2002 the popular SMARTER than JACK series has helped raise over NZ$280,000 for animal welfare charities. It is now helping animals in Canada, the United States, Australia, New Zealand and the United Kingdom.

The future of the SMARTER than JACK series holds a number of exciting books – there will be ones about cheeky animals, heroic animals and intuitive animals. You can subscribe to the series now too; more information can be found in the back of this book.

If you've had an amazing encounter with a smart animal we'd love to read about it. You may also like to sign up to receive the Story of the Week for a bit of inspiration – visit www.smarterthanjack.com

The enchanting cover photo

Masquerading behind the adoring expressions of our much loved pets are the stories and adventures, capers and escapades that have endeared them to our hearts and made them all a special part of the family.

This wonderful new edition of stories about everyday animals is brought to life with the enchanting cover photograph by renowned photographer Rachael Hale. Her distinctive images, famous around the world, capture the character and personality of her favourite friends, while allowing her to continue to support her favourite charity, the SPCA.

With the success of this series of animal anecdotes now established in New Zealand, Australia, Canada and soon the United Kingdom and United States, perhaps the best story is that the sale of every book makes a generous contribution to animal welfare in that country.

Rachael Hale Photography is proud to be associated with the SMARTER than JACK book series and trusts you'll enjoy these heart-warming stories that create such cherished images of our pets, along with the delightful pictures that tell such wonderful stories themselves.

David Todd
Rachael Hale Photography Limited
www.rachaelhale.com

The delightful illustrations

The lovely cat at the bottom of the pages in this book was drawn by Martin Wilkinson. Martin is a recent graduate from Massey University's Design School in Wellington, New Zealand where he majored in illustration. Martin is currently working on personal and freelance projects from a small but comfortable space at his kitchen table. He can be contacted by email at marlarkeee@gmail.com

Foreword: Useless? Who, me?

OK, so maybe it's a bad name. But it's been her name since she was born and I couldn't change it now. 'Useless': to everybody else, a shocking title; to me, my ginger and white housemate and buddy for the last seven and a half years.

People often say you're either a cat or dog person but I think there are definite animal people. I've had dogs, cats, sheep, fish and any number of small furries and loved them all. But most of them were family pets, whereas Useless is mine. Well, when I say mine, I mean she chooses to stay with me rather than move in with a neighbour.

In fact, many of my neighbours have tried on several occasions to coerce her into leaving me. Delicious food and fluffy beds have been laid on, cat

© Steve Leonard

Steve's good friend Useless

flaps fitted and attention lavished upon her. Even my own housemates and guests entice her onto their beds, convinced that she's there to stay. However, even though I spend a great deal of time travelling away from home, when I return she's right there on my bed with an innocent expression that seems to be saying, *What? Where've I been? What about you, where've you been?*

I know she misses me when I am away. The excited chirrups she makes when seeing me for the first time when I return are proof enough. And once, when I was away on a long trip and she was lodging with my mum, I happened to appear on the TV on an episode of *Vets in Practice*. My mum was sitting watching me on the telly when Useless came pelting in and started looking around the room for me. She could hear me but couldn't work out where I was.

Our relationship is not all a bed of roses. Many a time I have stretched a leg while half asleep and heard the thump of a cat hitting the floor. And, in return, what furniture I have is threadbare from scratching and covered in cat hairs. She's fallen out of two upstairs windows and, being a vet's cat, had needles and tablets thrust into her on a regular basis. Then there's the local wildlife issue. I am ashamed to say that as a younger thing she used to be into hunting – rabbits, mice, even bats (I told her it was illegal). So bells, curfews and chasing around the house to rescue captured prey were common occurrences. Many of her victims were rescued and released (including the bats – phew!) but some ended up inside that big furry belly. And so the biggest test of our friendship is just beginning – the diet!

But what would my home be without Useless? Without her little squeaks she makes when dreaming. Without the familiar weight of her body at the foot of the bed. Without the bang of the cat flap as she rushes in to see me.

Empty. That's what.

Steve Leonard
Cheshire
England

© Steve Leonard

About Steve Leonard

During the final year of his veterinary science degree at Bristol University Vet School, Steve Leonard agreed to participate in the filming of the BBC series *Vets' School*. The series was a huge success, and was followed by the popular *Vets in Practice*, which filmed Steve and other young vets as they went about their day-to-day working lives.

While working as a vet in Lancaster, Steve also presented *Vets in the Wild*. In September 1999, he gave up full-time veterinary employment and travelled all over the world filming *Steve Leonard's Ultimate Killers* with the BBC Natural History Unit.

Steve has now presented a number of BBC documentaries including *Steve Leonard's Extreme Animals*, *Animal Camera* and, more recently, *Journey of Life* in 2005.

1

Smart cats lend a paw

I'll show you where it is

Hamish, my cairn terrier, was a ball addict. I also had a tabby cat called Poppet.

Hamish would jump and catch the ball and bring it back to be thrown again – 24 hours a day if he could. But there was one ball and one only that he would play with. It was a small, rather hard, pink ball we had given him when he was a puppy. He loved that ball and had to have it with him at all times and in all places. He even took it to bed.

One day he took it into the garden and lost it. My husband and I searched high and low but no ball could be found. Hamish was devastated. He lay on the carpet, his tail drooping, and moped. This went on all day.

It was late afternoon when Poppet came in from the garden. She walked up to Hamish and meowed. He got up and followed her into the garden, and she showed him where she had found his ball.

Result: one ecstatic dog.

Mrs Lilian M Smith
Dobwalls, Cornwall
England

A cat with a mathematical bent

My husband's parents had a Siamese cat called Josie who loved to help in the vegetable garden.

Her talent shone through at planting time. She would watch the first few seedlings being planted out, and note the distance between each hole and the previous one. Then she would join in at the front of the advancing line, using her paw to make small holes exactly where each new plant would go.

The holes just had to be deepened a little and the plants could go in. Her help meant that whoever was planting could concentrate on the plant itself, rather than worry about alignment and spacing.

Wendy Willett
Russell Island, Queensland
Australia

Salem and his 'spider radar'

Spiders and I have an uneasy relationship. It used to be spider in one room, me in another, usually standing on a bed or cupboard, or hanging from a lampshade.

There's one thing worse than knowing a spider is in close proximity and that's *not* knowing a spider is there until it jumps on your head, runs up your leg or suddenly appears, all legs, over your shoulder. Obviously sensing my total terror – I think the blood-curdling screams gave me away – my cat Salem developed 'spider radar'. This took years of fine-tuning to develop.

As a kitten, Salem would stand in front of me, apparently protecting me, but as soon as the spider began to run straight at us, as all spiders inevitably do, we would both run in one direction or another. Salem could be found some time later, usually behind

Josie was very helpful in the garden

3

Salem helps maintain a 'spider-free' house

a curtain or on top of a tall bookcase. His bravery did not develop until he was a little bit older and a little bit bolder.

One glitch in the plan was the stage where Salem, now brave enough to confront the creature, would pick it up and spit it out on my lap. He soon learned this was not a good idea, as I would jump up and run screaming from the room.

Eventually my hero had it worked out:

1. Detect spider.

2. Chase it till cornered.

Then he looks to me to finish the job. Quavering in my boots, I cover the beastie with a glass and slide a piece of cardboard underneath it. I pick it up, hoping and praying the spider doesn't have superhero powers and can break free at any time. Quickly I open the door and put it as far away as my bravery will take me, then run back to my house. Finally, Salem and I nod to each other at a job well done.

Sometimes Salem is a little bit too smart and occasionally tricks me by going into 'spider radar' for a fictional spider. I do the motions with shaking glass and quivering card, only to find I've spent half an hour trying to catch a piece of fluff. Salem just sits, smiling smugly. I still reward him with a big hug and kiss because he's my hero.

Diane Burgess
Bordesley Green, Birmingham
England

Look what I found!

My two cats Ronnie and Scamp look quite ordinary, but when I tell you of Scamp's abilities you will be astounded.

Scamp had lost his collar while he was outside and, as I had just bought him a new ID tag, I was quite upset. To my amazement, a few days later the collar and ID tag turned up on my back doorstep. I was somewhat sceptical about a cat's ability to find its own collar and carry it home, but I replaced the collar on Scamp and thought no more about it.

Some time later, Ronnie came home minus his collar and tag. This time I was convinced that they had gone for good, but, much to my surprise, what did I receive on my doorstep again a few days later but Ronnie's collar and tag, with Scamp standing beside them looking very proud of himself.

And I thought it was only dogs that were supposed to be clever!

Mrs A P Smart
Billericay, Essex
England

5

The kitten who wouldn't wash

One evening a few years ago a black cat turned up, filthy and starving, on the doorstep of the house-turned-into-flats where I lived.

I opened the door to let myself in, and he walked ahead of me and headed straight down the stairs to my basement flat as if he knew exactly where to go. He could just as easily have gone upstairs to the upper-floor flats. I called him Peri.

One day a friend gave me a homeless ginger kitten. She couldn't keep it as she was asthmatic with a strong allergy to cats. I called him Rufus and hoped Peri would accept him as part of the household. Peri showed his displeasure by ignoring both the kitten and me.

Rufus was younger than he appeared, for he didn't have a clue about washing himself. I tried butter on his paws, a sprinkle of water across his back and even sponging him with a damp cloth, but nothing worked. One day, as I was setting out to do some shopping, I said to Peri, 'That kitten must absolutely *stink* to you, because he just won't wash. I do wish you'd try and teach him.'

When I came back, both cats were – unusually – sitting side by side, bolt upright, in the middle of the living room carpet. Rufus was absolutely spotless, so much so that I discovered he had pale cream fur, which had never been visible before, ringing his eyes. I believe Peri had pinned Rufus down and washed him thoroughly – and maybe he insisted that Rufus wash himself properly from then on.

From that day forward, Rufus washed himself like any normal cat. Indeed, he and Peri became the best of friends and often groomed each other.

P M Shaw-Brookman
St Pancras, London
England

Monty the retriever

My cat Monty, who is a twin, liked to explore the gardens around our house. He came in one day minus his collar and identity disc.

I was upset that he had lost it, and looked everywhere. I decided to get another one made up for him the following day.

I think he knew something was missing, for the next day he came in through the cat flap, the collar in his mouth. He dropped it at my feet.

Another time I lost my gold chain while I was gardening, and gave it up for lost. A few weeks later Monty trotted in, my chain in his mouth, and dropped it at my feet. He must have dug it up, as it was covered in mud. Since then, we've had many other bits and pieces brought inside.

Mrs D Snook
Bishops Stortford, Hertfordshire
England

Clever Monty (right) and twin brother Sox

7

So you'd like me to find her?

My daughter was moving house so I kept her kittens, Tinkerbell and Naughty, in my own house while she packed up, moved into the new home and got settled in. My own cat, five-year-old Mona, tolerated them and they behaved well.

One morning Naughty went missing. The visiting cats weren't allowed outside, so where could she be?

I live in a three-storey house with many rooms. I called Mona and she came to sit on the coffee table; I sat in front of her on the settee. I looked straight at her and said, 'I cannot find that little kitten, I've looked everywhere but I can't find her.'

Mona jumped off the coffee table and went downstairs. Upstairs are the bedrooms, whose doors are kept shut. Cats get to roam on the middle floor, upstairs, and downstairs into a basement flat which has two spare rooms and a bathroom. A few minutes later, Mona came back and meowed at me, in that way which seems to say, *Come with me*. She took a couple of steps, looked back at me as if to say, *Are you coming?* and meowed again.

I followed, and she took me into the front spare room. She jumped onto a table and looked up. Halfway up the window (the old-fashioned type with sash cords) sat Naughty, too frightened to move.

I took her down, praised Mona no end and gave her some treats.

Mrs P Maddams
Plaistow, London
England

2

Smart cats take control

Stop that noise, will you?

One evening I was practising a piece of music which I was to sing in a choir selection.

Simon, my chocolate point Siamese cat, ran into the room. He looked at me strangely, gave three or four short meows and left again. Once more I proceeded to sing (and, let me tell you, it was not a high-pitched piece or anything like that), and once more Simon came on the run into the room. This time he climbed onto my lap and stared at me nose to nose, as if to say, *That's enough.*

By this time I was laughing so hard that, just for the heck of it, I started up again with my singing. Again he came dashing in, but this time he did not look me in the face. Instead, he nipped my hand as if to tell me, *Shut up already, I've heard enough.*

He is fine with the radio and tapes or CDs but my singing does it for him.

He came to us as a stray and is a perfect gentleman around our other cat, Midnite, letting him eat, drink and enter the house first. He is indeed a real character.

Cheryl Schopff
Kindersley, Saskatchewan
Canada

9

Simon made sure Cheryl knew exactly what he thought of her singing

Come on, have a look at my baby

Our cat Marcus seemed to fancy the cat two houses away from us. She was always flirting with him, and he made her pregnant.

My friend Elle, who lived four doors down, asked me to come round and look at the new kittens; she said they were definitely like my cat Marcus. Two were black with white paws and a white diamond, just like him.

Time went by and I still hadn't been to see them. One Sunday morning I opened my back door to see Marcus coming down the path with something in his mouth. He often brought presents of mice or birds to put at our feet or on the mat, so I thought grumpily, 'Oh, what's that darned cat caught this time?'

As he drew closer, I could see a tiny black kitten in his mouth. He placed it gently at my feet and stood back, as if to say, *I am so proud of my baby – there, look what I've done.*

Then he carefully scooped up the little bundle and took it back to its mother.

Patricia Rose Ribbits (née Sweeney)
Dymchurch, Kent
England

Mandy had a strict code of conduct

We couldn't resist those gigantic eyes and massive ears plastered on the tiniest body we had ever seen. She was black as midnight, and sprinkled with a handful of dust bunnies. We brought the stray kitten home to be part of our growing feline family. We didn't know she'd wandered into our lives for a purpose.

Mandy was terrified of loud kitchen appliances, obnoxious pets and even the people who had saved her from homelessness. But, after all, she had been left to fend for herself. With time and affection, she developed a big heart and was quick to return our devotion and friendship.

But she was no pushover. We liked to think of her as our little mother, doling out abundant love but, at the same time, setting boundaries for our behaviour. Mandy was in charge. She had a strict code of conduct that she expected us to follow, and she made it clear soon enough.

We discovered that Mandy despised shouting. In fact, it was her one unbending maternal rule: no screaming, no yelling, no hollering. Coincidentally, my sisters and I spent a great deal of time quarrelling. Mandy simply wouldn't put up with it. One way or another, we were

11

in trouble. When we disregarded the rule, Mandy climbed into our laps or paced around our feet, crying non-stop until we suspended our shouting match. She was relentless.

Mandy knew there was no room for animosity in our family. Where did sharp retorts and sarcastic words get us in the long run? It was as though she knew it was futile and she would do anything to get her point across. Somehow, hearing it from Mandy was more palatable than hearing it from our own mother. Her unwavering opinion made us laugh and, in the end, made us reconcile.

Yes, some relationships are important to hold onto. Mandy gave us that wake-up call.

Annette Gulati
Round Rock, Texas
United States

You've gone to the wrong house!

In the 1940s, when I was a young child, my family had a large black and white cat called Sammy. We thought that he was the cleverest, kindest cat in the world.

In those days, car engines were noisy and no two cars seemed to make the same sound. We lived part-way down a hill, and my father would drive up to the top of the hill, turn the car around and come down again in order to park in front of the house. Sammy would hear the engine, jump into my father's chair and pretend to be sleeping deeply. When my father entered the house, no matter how many times we told him what the cat had done, my dad would sit on the footstool by his chair and offer many apologies and lots of affection before taking the cat off the chair.

My father was a medical practitioner in our small town and in those days doctors made house calls. One day our next-door neighbour needed medical attention. On his way home from the office, my father stopped at the neighbour's house. Soon he saw Sammy sitting on the windowsill outside the neighbour's house and heard him howling loudly. When my father emerged from the house, Sammy led him down to our house. As they walked, Sammy kept scolding him and turning back as if to check that this man – who had made such a stupid mistake by going to the wrong house – was following his cat, who knew better.

Sammy was protective of us, just like a dog. At our cottage we had an outhouse and he would accompany my sister and me whenever we needed the outhouse at night. The cottage was on the edge of a small lake and we had a small battery-powered boat. Whenever we went out in that boat, Sammy would pace along the shore following us and seemed to be scolding us for being so foolish.

What an amazing cat! We remember his many smart ideas – even now, so many years later!

Lynda Nanders
Etobicoke, Ontario
Canada

Henry the bookshop cat

'That little ginger cat – he's there again.'

From the window of our bookshop in the market town of Bakewell – famous for its puddings – we'd watched it scampering around, dodging traffic, and appearing and disappearing as cats are prone to do. The traffic is continual and heavy, and we feared for its safety.

13

It seemed healthy and we enquired to whom it belonged but no one knew. The owners of the local pet shop told us it visited them daily. They would hide 'cat nips' and watch it find them every time. What a clever little streetwise puss.

In the back of our office, our two red setters, Flame and Polly, lazed on their comfy cushions behind a half stable door. On one particularly hot summer day, the little cat ran into our shop – and our lives.

The dogs watched with amazement as it leaped in and proceeded to drink their water. Frightened by Flame's startled barking, the cat retreated. But one afternoon soon afterwards, when the town overflowed with visitors and holidaymakers, a customer said, 'Do you know there's a cat sleeping in your window?' Actually, we *had* wondered why half of Bakewell had suddenly taken such an interest in the works of Shakespeare and Dylan Thomas. We peeped – and there was ginger puss, curled up and basking in the sunshine alongside, of all things, the children's book *Ten Little Pussy Cats*.

That Christmas we had to take our customary Christmas stable from the window when someone remarked, 'It makes a change to have a real live cat lying in the straw instead of the usual donkey.' Our little friend had become a regular visitor, enjoying the fuss and attention, while we shared our counter with a curled-up cat. But we feared for his safety on the road and decided to contact his owner.

Around his neck was a disc: 'I am Henry cat. My phone number is —.' We visited his family, a nice couple at the top of Bakewell who owned two other cats. These two wouldn't venture outside, whereas Henry wouldn't stay in. Louise, Henry's owner, said he always escaped, no matter how she tried to confine him. It was a little while before we discovered *how* he escaped.

In their cellar was an old air-grate with bars, on view to the street. Henry had learned to climb up and meow pitifully to passers-by.

Henry made himself at home in the bookshop

They naturally thought, 'The poor cat is stuck', and proceeded to let him out once again.

Henry had a love affair with our shop. Granted, we fed him – well, how could we have such a loving and loyal guest and *not* offer him refreshments? Not only did he visit while the shop was open, he was there every morning. We would arrive to find him sitting on the pavement outside the locked door, waiting for us.

Louise would say, 'It's too early, Henry, they're not open yet', but nothing deterred him. Sometimes we arrived at the same time: John, Flame, Polly and me, and – wandering around the corner, tail held high, purring and meowing his *Good morning* – Henry. 'Good morning, Henry,' we'd respond as we opened the door. '*He* certainly knows where he's going,' many a passer-by would remark.

But the road grew more dangerous. We would hear the *peep, peep* of the crossing adjacent to our doorway. The traffic stopped and Henry would walk across along with the pedestrians. No harm must come to him, for by now Henry had captured and captivated our hearts.

So each evening after we closed, we would drive the cat home in our car. We'd pull up, hoot the horn and pass him through the car window into Louise's waiting arms, to be securely restrained until morning when the whole procedure would begin again.

One day Henry resolved the situation for himself. The postman left our letter box open and, as it was a large one, Henry assumed that we had installed his own personal cat flap. We'd get there to find him already inside the shop, awaiting his breakfast.

His family was moving house. They dared not take Henry, knowing he would simply walk back to us, with even more roads to negotiate. He had previously gone missing for three months before being found in a nearby village. He had climbed onto the last bus to Matlock and was collected from the bus depot at midnight.

So would we like to keep him? We would indeed.

He has settled down, and seems content to lie around with our dogs during the daytime, and play with them at night while we clean the shop. Flame and Polly are no longer with us, but Henry has now befriended young Polly, Marcus, Monty and Poppy.

He sleeps on sheepskin cushions on our shop counter. He turned 12 in 2005, eight years after he first ran into our shop. Like us he's growing older, but he seems happy to live the life he chose for himself. We're ever thankful for the first day we saw him on the streets of Bakewell, and grateful that he chose to stay with us.

Mrs Wendy Moncrieff
Bakewell, Derbyshire
England

> Write to me ... ✉
>
> Wendy Moncrieff
> 'Avenall', 18 Wyedale Crescent
> Bakewell, Derbyshire
> DE45 1BE
> United Kingdom

City-smart cat and squirrel

It started when we saw a squirrel in our backyard looking for food before winter. We tapped on the window as we threw bread out for it. Even over the winter, Psycho Joe the squirrel – named by my daughter – would return on the nicer days, often staying by the back fence until we would tap on the glass for him to get his treat.

I'd spend time watching him walk the wires of power lines and fence tops like roadways. Psycho Joe would jump to our garage, leap to a branch of our silver maple and scurry quickly to the back sliding glass door for his treat. I always told our cat Midnight that he wasn't to chase the squirrel, only to make sure it didn't get inside.

17

We often hand-fed Psycho Joe a few peanuts. He took them gently out of my hand as the cat watched beside me. Psycho Joe would turn the nut around. If it was perfect he'd go and bury it, then come back for another treat, and if the shell was damaged he'd sit and eat it there with Midnight not ten inches away. How he knew he was safe I'll never know. He often waited to cross to my yard until he saw my car pull in after dropping my three kids off at school.

On one occasion I forgot to leave peanuts on the porch. I heard the cat crying and fussing by the sliding door and there was Psycho Joe sitting on the step tapping on the glass, looking and waiting for his treat. On another occasion when I wasn't quick enough hand-feeding Psycho Joe he stuck his head in the door, and Midnight (being a brave watch cat) gave Psycho Joe a tap on the head with his paw – just enough to say, *Back up*. He didn't even use his claws. Psycho Joe backed up, looking apologetic, and waited for his nut. I think that indicates both a smart cat and a smart squirrel, although a stupid owner – one should never feed wild animals, as it is dangerous because of diseases and it fosters unnatural eating habits in wildlife.

D Lauck-Putnoky
United States

BR the 'practice' cat

While I was in practice as a veterinary surgeon some years ago, we were presented with an emergency case. A tabby cat had been found on the railway line, badly injured.

She was in a sorry state but survived the initial shock, and we carried out emergency treatment while waiting for her owners to claim her. In view of where she was found, the nurses gave her the temporary name BR (British Rail), as that's how the railways were known at the time.

She had to have one eye removed and a leg amputated but made a remarkable recovery. In spite of much advertising, no one came to claim her. We all became very fond of her and there was no way we could put her to sleep. But nor could we find a suitable home for her, so we decided to keep her as the 'practice' cat.

At first we thought she'd have to live indefinitely in a hospital cage. BR had very different ideas and soon had free run of the practice.

She soon showed us what she expected of us, and if she could get into the waiting room she would defy any dog to move her from where she was, or wanted to be. She sat on the appointments book or the credit card machine in reception, and resented having to move if they were required.

She also liked the sample bags of food which we had on display for clients. If she felt hungry, BR would open a bag. Unfortunately, once she'd had one meal from a bag, she preferred to open another one the next time she was hungry.

We came to realise it was a very good thing to have her about the practice for clients to see. Of course, sometimes she decided to go outside to climb a tree or sit in the sun, but, if people saw her when they visited the practice, they weren't as horrified or upset as they might have been should their own animal need the type of surgery she had had. They could see that BR was very happy despite losing both an eye and a leg.

As it happened, she lost her tail as well. Several years after her first accident, she went into the car park one day. She did this regularly and would refuse to move for cars, even if they hooted at her. At the end of one consulting period she returned with a tail so badly injured that it had to be amputated. Presumably she'd refused to move for a car and it had run over her tail. When she came in that day, she

19

didn't go into reception as usual but sat outside the operating theatre door and meowed to go in.

She was already adult when she arrived at the practice but we had her for a further 12 years. Everyone was very sorry when she eventually had to be put to sleep, and for a long time afterwards our clients would ask after her when they came in.

Heather Briggs
Port Solent, Portsmouth, Hampshire
England

A Siamese to be reckoned with

A chocolate point Siamese, Coco was the runt of the litter but had the biggest personality. She was basically an indoor cat, allowed outside only for short periods when we were home, and always kept in at night.

She loved her excursions but would never wander too far away. She'd often come flying up the yard, along the deck, in the door and through the house to her litter tray. Moments later, she'd stroll back outside to continue exploring whatever had been rudely interrupted by a call of nature.

One evening she was staring at a moth which had landed high up on the lounge room wall. She tried to jump up but it was just out of her reach. And then, just like in the cartoons, we could almost see a light bulb appear above her head. She took off through the kitchen into the laundry, where she jumped up on the ironing board, permanently set up against the same wall that backed onto the lounge room wall.

She'd apparently worked out that if she jumped onto the ironing board she'd be able to reach the moth. When our laughter subsided she reluctantly returned, but ignored both the moth and us for the rest of the evening.

Several dogs learned that she was not to be trifled with and that their size meant nothing. One German shepherd was undoubtedly glad we had a flyscreen door. He arrived with visiting friends, but when Coco saw the dog at the back door she flew up the passage, leaped up at full force and landed with all four feet and claws hanging on the flywire of the door.

Another friend brought his Great Dane over. He left it sitting in the car, whereupon Coco jumped on the vehicle and paced all around the bonnet, roof and boot, trying to find a way in.

Someone else claimed that cats never attack a target that doesn't move. He held his hand out in front of her and kept it still. Coco blew that theory. She lived until she was 18 and we love to tell our children stories of her many exploits.

Pam Moorfoot
Geelong, Victoria
Australia

A feline chaperone

Our cat Pixie was just eight weeks old when we got her, and at first she wasn't allowed outside unless accompanied by me or the children. I taught her the word 'walkies' and before long she would run to the door when she heard it.

Eventually I let her out on her own, and she started following us wherever we went. She would go with us when we went swimming and would wait patiently outside the pool for an hour and a half, then walk home with us. She would go to school with the children, and sit at the school gates waiting for them.

21

One evening we were at school to see my eldest son's Year 6 show. We were among the audience when a teacher shouted out for the 'cat lady'. Pixie had ventured into the school building. If no one knew me before that night, they certainly did afterwards.

I rang the vet for advice and was told Pixie might have 'behavioural problems'. I told them I'd had three years' training as a counsellor – would I do? A mental image crept into my mind of Pixie lying on her back, legs crossed, telling me all her problems. When I told the school of her diagnosis, they offered to place her in the special needs class.

These days, when I get a phone call from the school, it's usually because Pixie is trying to get into the building. I risk life and limb running into the road in order to chase her away from oncoming cars. If I shut her in the house when I go out, she finds a window open upstairs and jumps out so that she can be with us.

One day I let her out an hour or so before I was due to fetch the children from school. When I left the house I expected her to catch up and follow me, but, as I turned the corner, she was already well in front of me, going off to school on her own as if she knew it was home time.

People who see our faithful, loyal cat following us think it's sweet. We think she's more of a liability. But we wouldn't be without her.

Joanne Candlin
Hartsholme, Lincoln
England

Pixie took top prize in a 2004 *Lincolnshire Echo* Cat Tales competition. The judges were impressed with her chaperoning skills.

Jake the food critic

Heat up my food, please!

My two cats Jake and Hobo are aged 10 and 15. They constantly amaze me with their ability to prove how smart they are by skilfully communicating their needs and wishes. The following is one such example.

Jake had been to the vet for a minor procedure. Upon his arrival home, his appetite was a bit lacking. To enhance his cat food's taste and smell, I warmed it gently in the microwave oven. This renewed Jake's interest in eating and so I warmed his canned food again the next day. He was enjoying his food, his appetite had returned and his recovery was complete.

The following morning, knowing Jake was now fine, I presented his cat food cold from the refrigerator as usual. Jake walked over to his bowl, and sniffed and eyed his food with much disdain. In a very determined manner he crossed the kitchen floor, sat firmly under the microwave oven and, with a wide-eyed stare and a loud outraged meow, told me in no uncertain terms that I had neglected to warm his cat food! Both my mother and I knew without question what Jake was requesting. Well trained as I am, I retrieved his dish and warmed his food, and Jake happily ate his meal. I'm still warming his food!

Barbara Tillmann Jones
Bayfield, Ontario
Canada

> Write to me ... ✉
>
> Barbara Tillmann Jones
> PO Box 243
> Bayfield ON N0M 1G0
> Canada

Are you satisfied now?

I was walking past the end of our kitchen one morning when I met our cat Fluff coming down from the other end of the room where I'd given him his breakfast.

I looked past him to the remains of his meal and was annoyed to see that he had deposited a large part of it on the floor around his dish, which is always a bone of contention between us.

'What's that!' I roared, pointing accusingly down the room. He immediately did an about-turn, stalked back to the dish and cleaned up the offending bits of cat food. Then he trotted outside, giving me an oh-so-virtuous look as he passed by. Did I hear him say, *Fussy old bag! Now are you satisfied?*

Margaret Moje
Waipu, Northland
New Zealand

3

Smart cats take care of others

My 'hearing cat'

I am very hard of hearing, but it was only when my husband died over 20 years ago that my tortoiseshell cat Topsy took it upon herself to become my hearing cat for the deaf.

Whenever the telephone rang she would meow very loudly and stare fixedly at it until I answered it. This was repeated whenever there was someone at the door. She never made a mistake, and continued to do it for many years until she herself became deaf and partially sighted.

Of course, I shall never know whether she realised I couldn't hear the sound or whether she simply wanted it to stop. No matter – she helped me.

Sadly, I had to have Topsy put to sleep in 2004 at the grand old age of 23. To me she will always be special.

P Fitzpatrick
Chapeltown, Sheffield
England

Tigger became a mother figure

When Tigger was three we decided to get another cat. In one litter we looked at were two long-haired kittens. There had originally been three but one had died, and one of the remaining two was very ill. We decided on the healthy one, but our hearts wouldn't let us leave the sick one behind so we took him too. We named them Jerusalem and Jericho.

Our vet told us that Jericho had almost no chance of survival. He was getting weaker every day, since Jerusalem was easily able to take food from him.

When we thought all hope was lost, Tigger became a mother figure to Jericho. He guarded him while he was eating, and made sure Jerusalem did not take his food. He washed him, and kept him in his bed by snuggling up with him. As a result of Tigger's work, Jericho thrived and proved the vet wrong. Both cats lived until they were 15.

Caitlin Loughran
Portrush, County Antrim
Northern Ireland

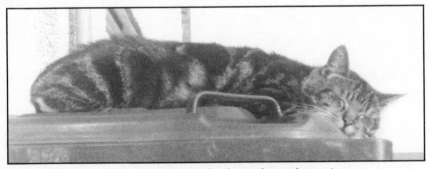

Tigger takes a well-deserved break from his mothering duties

Hang on, I'll fetch my friends

My son, who is a chef, was working on a wedding feast. The chefs were outside the marquee for a break while the guests ate the course they'd just served.

A cat came along and went through the usual pantomime of wanting food. One of the chefs went inside and brought out a fillet steak – which the guests were enjoying – cut up on a piece of paper. The cat began to eat and soon ran off, but swiftly returned, accompanied by four of its mates. They all tucked into their succulent and unexpected meal.

Mrs Stella Bond
Winchester, Hampshire
England

Tinkerbell was my one link to sanity

I was born in Borrigone, not far from Limerick and close to the banks of the River Shannon in Eire. I came to England at the age of three and was placed in a boys' home in Coleshill near Birmingham.

Run by nuns and priests, the home housed more than 400 kids aged between one and 16. It was a very tough home, with no niceties such as birthdays or Christmas presents. Just the basics to keep going. I had always assumed I was an orphan and only discovered the truth years later. As you can imagine, love and affection were nowhere to be seen.

Enter Tinkerbell. She was my one link to sanity in an insane kaleidoscopic world of struggling to make sense of what was going on. Tinkerbell was a large fluffy black and white stray cat who wandered into the home one day and sat on my lap. Those responsible for us

27

tried to get rid of her but I raised merry hell; I was uncontrollable at the grand age of five. Eventually they allowed the cat to come and go as she pleased.

I gave Tinkerbell meat treats, cooked bacon or cheese whenever we had them. I would sneak out of bed at 2 or 3 am and raid the kitchen to get her a decent titbit. Actually she was an excellent mouser – there was many a time when she'd bring prey inside and lie down under my bed for a good feast. All I could hear were the crunching sounds of bone cracking, and loud purrs.

Tinkerbell went with me on long walks in the countryside, and never once went off on her own. She followed me to school and always waited for me to return. For some unknown reason, nobody bothered me when Tinkerbell was around. She would sleep on my bed at night, purring and giving me slow blinks. It was wonderful having something to hold onto and to love, at a time when such things were thought unnecessary.

There came a time when she didn't turn up, and instinctively I knew that she would never turn up again. It was probably one of the saddest days of my life. Tinkerbell had been with me for a grand total of ten years.

She gave me love and affection, and without her I do not think I would be the person I am today. All in all, I was the lucky one. I don't look back with sadness at my upbringing. Instead, I celebrate what I achieved by getting through it and surviving it all – with the help of Tinkerbell, a fluffy black and white stray moggie.

Padraig
Wednesfield, Wolverhampton
England

Smudge seemed to understand how Chris was feeling

Smudge came to comfort me

I have ME and one night I had been feeling rather low.

My cat Smudge heard me having a good old wail. He came to me and placed his paw on my hand. It made such a difference to me and I'll never forget it. I know it's not a remarkable story, but for my cat to understand how I was feeling and to empathise was really quite remarkable to me. He looked at me with such an intense gaze that I'm sure he wanted to connect with me in his own way.

He was originally a stray cat, had never done this before and isn't really a 'lap cat' so it was all the more extraordinary.

Mrs Chris Southworth
Llandudno, Conwy
Wales

29

My cats saved a kitten

My cats Marcie and Domingo slipped past the hedge, two shadows lost in the wind. They darted in and out of a bush in a zigzag, and then raced up the stone steps and strutted elegantly in front of the door. The door opened and a hand reached down and stroked them. The cats purred affectionately as two bowls of food were placed on the step. They gulped it down and seemed to exchange smiles, as if thinking how easily a human can be tricked. Then once more they set off into the night.

The following day they returned cold, hungry and soaking wet. I dried and fed them. Then they started trying desperately to get my attention. I had been tripped up and headbutted several times before I finally realised they wanted me to follow them.

They led me down to the nearby stream. Lying on the sand was a tiny black and grey kitten.

It seems my cats had found him near death on the riverside. They had stayed nursing him overnight and came to get my help in the morning.

I named the kitten 'Tiny' and took him to the SPCA that afternoon. He now has his own family and couldn't be happier – thanks to my smart cats. I now make sure I give my cats a little extra food every night.

Kape Sinnott
Queenstown
New Zealand

Heroic siblings – Marcie (top) and Domingo

Sylvester grew up to become a hero

Our cat Socks had been missing for several days. She was about to have kittens so I checked out all her known hidey-holes but she wasn't in any of them.

Eventually I tried the shed. It was filled with old furniture, cardboard cartons full of junk and empty tea chests. I moved broken chairs and a rickety old table out of the way and started to look through the chests, but after an hour of moving boxes from one place to another I was exhausted.

I sat on an upturned box and fanned myself with a piece of cardboard I'd accidentally ripped off one of the boxes. Then I thought I heard a faint mewing. I held my breath in case it was just me wheezing from all the dust, but I heard it again – and it seemed to come from all the tea chests at once!

Finally I found Socks and her kittens. They were in one of the bottom tea chests and I assume that, when the cat jumped into one, those on top must have teetered back and forth and then fallen back onto her tea chest, shutting her in. She was so weak she couldn't stand up, but with love and care she and her three kittens not only survived but thrived.

I named the black and white kitten Sylvester after the cartoon character, and he became a champion mouse catcher. This was just as well, as the area around Ouyen – where I lived at the time – was slap bang in the middle of a mouse plague. If you've never experienced a mouse plague, let me enlighten you. For a start, the smell is something you'll never forget. It seems to stay in your nostrils for life. And the sight of thousands upon thousands of mice moving as one is incredible. It looks like a massive grey blanket moving across the ground of its own accord.

Our hen house was awash with mice. They'd leap into the pail of grain I was holding to feed the chooks, and start eating from it.

Other mice would eat the grain even before it hit the ground. The poor chooks were upset, as not only did the mice pinch their food but they also fouled their drinking water. They pooped in it and some mice even drowned in it. The smell of dead and decaying mice was overpowering.

Inside our house we didn't fare much better. I'd put a pillow over my head at night so that I wouldn't hear the sound of mousetraps going off in rapid succession, one after the other, as soon as we'd gone to bed. I was also very uneasy about putting my foot straight onto the floor when I got out of bed, in case I stepped on a mouse. I even had to check my slippers before I put them on, in case a mouse had decided they'd make a cosy place to give birth to a family in.

Farmers pleaded with us town folk to give up our cats to them so that they could put them to work killing the mice in their sheds and paddocks. My mother gave away Socks and another female, along with their latest litters. She gave Sylvester and his siblings to my sister Yvonne who had just married a farmer, Les. That left us with only Sandy, a much loved but useless ginger tomcat. He was so terrified of mice he used to jump onto the kitchen table and scream at them until we came along to chase them away. The only way Sandy would ever have caught a mouse would have been if one crawled into his mouth during one of his hourly siestas and he accidentally swallowed it.

The mouse plague finally ended, the way they always do. The mice turned on each other and before long most of them were dead. About a year later, Yvonne and Les became the proud parents of a baby boy they named Graham. He was born with a cleft palate and needed constant attention.

One day when he was about six months old, Yvonne left him in his bouncer on the back veranda while she hung out the washing.

33

The phone rang and she went inside to answer it. She was delayed for some minutes taking the call, when she heard a commotion from the back veranda and Graham's shrill cries. She dropped the phone and raced outside, and what she saw stunned her.

Sylvester was in mortal combat with a brown snake, right next to Graham. Yvonne grabbed a broom and whacked the snake until it went limp. Only then did she see that Sylvester was staggering about, gasping. It turned out that the snake had repeatedly bitten him, but the brave little cat didn't release his grip until Yvonne came out and killed the snake. Then he died.

I've often wondered what would have happened to Graham if Sylvester hadn't been there to save him. What if he had died in that tea chest along with his mother and siblings? Would Graham have been bitten by the snake and died? Or would there have been a 'plan B'? I'll never know. I'm just thankful that Sylvester was there and that he was brave enough to take the snake on.

Carole Lawrence
Canberra, ACT
Australia

Lily was my nurse

The day I met Lily, my beloved Alabaster had been found dead in the garden. We'd let him out the night before and he didn't come back when he was called. My partner and I were devastated. I had to get another cat – not to replace Alabaster but to have something to love and focus on. We visited a local cat rescue place, where several rescue cats came up to us as if to say *Pick me*, but Lily just wanted to run and hide. I knew straight away she needed us as much as we needed her so we took her home.

Lily cured Helen's headache

She wouldn't leave her bed, and tried to bury her head so she wouldn't be seen. Every evening I would keep her bed on my lap, talking softly and stroking her, until with patience and plenty of TLC she came out of her shell. Now she rules the roost.

About a year ago, I developed a really bad headache. Painkillers wouldn't touch it and I became so distressed I was in tears and didn't know what to do with myself. Lily climbed onto my lap and began

35

to push her head into my face and make a strange noise. My partner kept putting her on the floor, but she was insistent and continued the ritual until my head felt better. Fortunately it was nothing serious, although I was checked over in casualty.

Lily has never made that noise or been as pushy since, but she seems to know my moods. When I'm feeling down – for instance, when I had to have one of my dogs put down – she doesn't leave my side.

Helen Hurkett
Penzance, Cornwall
England

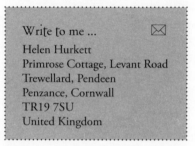

Write to me ...

Helen Hurkett
Primrose Cottage, Levant Road
Trewellard, Pendeen
Penzance, Cornwall
TR19 7SU
United Kingdom

Oliver was trying to say something

Paola was alone at home, feeling depressed as usual. Her illness was really getting her down.

She was only 60 but already had difficulty walking, kept losing her balance and felt tired all the time. She was sick and tired, and the worst part of her illness was not being able to hear properly. People had to speak very close to her, almost into her ear, or she wouldn't hear what they said. She could hardly have a proper conversation and had given up listening to music and going to the theatre. It only made her nervous and sad, not being able to enjoy it fully.

Goodbye to Andrew Lloyd Webber, the Beatles and Elton John. Paola often felt like crying, and didn't know what made her keep struggling and going on with such a miserable life.

Standing by the sink, she saw Oliver, her gorgeous tabby, and knew there was at least one answer to that question. She and her husband Silio hadn't wanted him at first but now they adored him. Paola hadn't liked cats at all for a long time, and her husband had been the same. They thought of cats as selfish animals, only capable of asking for food and a place to sleep, and loving their house much more than they loved their owners.

Oliver was the neighbours' cat but they didn't like him – they left him alone and treated him badly. Paola and Silio didn't approve; they felt a pet shouldn't be treated like that once he'd been adopted.

Oliver understood their true nature, and one day he showed up at their kitchen door, meowing, weary, hungry and lonely. It was enough to move them.

Talk about being clever! The first move had been made and he was allowed inside. After that, Oliver gained their love step by step and turned into their adored little king. He was always there for a cuddle when they were sad, always near them when they were ill.

Now he was looking at Paola with eyes wide open, as if he were trying to say something. He turned his back and went into the next room, only to come back again, look at her and turn away – again and again and again, until Paola decided to follow him.

As she approached the table on which the phone had been placed, she heard a faint ring she hadn't been able to hear from the sink. She picked up the receiver. 'Hello?' Oliver looked satisfied and turned away as if he'd said, *I've done my bit.*

'Mum, where were you? I was beginning to get worried.'

'Worried about me?' Paola smiled. 'Not as long as my clever, helpful Oliver is here.'

37

'Oliver? What do you mean? He didn't answer the phone, did he?'

'Well, he almost did. And you know what I think? This amazing cat would be able to call for help himself if I needed it!'

'Mum, are you sure you're feeling OK?'

Paola was sure she was feeling a little bit safer with Oliver there. He was now peacefully sleeping in his basket.

By the way, the story's true. And Paola's my mum.

C Giuntini
Prato
Italy

Safe keeping

I moved house when Millie Muppet was a year old. I hadn't been able to have her neutered, so a very pregnant cat went with me to an old cottage near a small village green. It was a peaceful safe haven for pets.

A month later she gave birth to two huge ginger toms and a tiny bundle of black fur with a huge white ruff whom I called Polly Pocket. She kept them upstairs in a cupboard next to my bed, finally allowing the nesting box to be taken downstairs.

One day when the kittens were about five weeks old, there was a thunderstorm. The lightning was scary and the thunder deafening. I hurried to the box in the hallway where Millie had been nursing her kittens. The box was empty.

I searched the house frantically but found no sign of them. The back door had been left open to cool the house before the storm, so I ran out into the garden in teeming rain, calling for Millie.

Millie Muppet found a safe place for her kittens

My neighbours joined in, and we spent half an hour searching the garden. Finally, soaked and bedraggled, we went back inside.

I was convinced the kittens had run off in fright and were lost forever. Near to tears, I put the kettle on for my friends, trying not to think of the poor mites, lost and crying for their mother. Just then I heard a bump and a plaintive meow.

Millie was coming down the stairs, dragging Polly by the scruff of her neck. She stalked over to the nesting box and dropped Polly unceremoniously inside before heading upstairs again. I followed and was overjoyed to find she'd hidden the kittens at the back of the bedroom cupboard where they'd lived when they were first born. I heard indignant cries as the boys waited for their mum to take them out. I could have cried with relief.

More recently, I organised a petition to the local council, asking for parking restrictions on the main road to which we exit from

our unadopted road. One freezing November night I plucked up courage to knock on doors in the hope of getting signatures from equally concerned residents. It was a bit nerve-racking, but I needn't have worried for I had the best icebreaker I could ask for.

Millie followed me to every house and soon had the round sorted: find the short cut and sit on the doorstep ahead of me. When the resident opened the door, Millie would be looking at them as if to say, *Come on, hurry up, it's cold out here!*

The final call was to a house in the next road and I thought Millie had given up and gone home. As I made my way to the front door, I heard a familiar bell tinkling. The security lights went on and Millie was the only creature at the front door when it opened. Luckily, Gerry thought it highly amusing and readily agreed to sign the petition, as had everyone else we'd approached.

Mrs Noelle Orton
Chestfield, Kent
England

Write to me ... ✉
email Noelle
g.wooduk@virgin.net

A feline nurse

Tinkerbell infuriated me ... but she cured me – of migraines, of anything she could.

For the 19 years of her life, Tinkerbell believed I had to be looked after.

When migraines clamped down, the pain driving me to a dark room for the day, Tink came too. She'd curl up next to me, staying until the pain left, often leaving just as it subsided.

One day I wrenched the muscles in my back. The pain was unbelievable. I don't know how I did it, whether lifting heavy boxes or just twisting the wrong way, but I was in agony. I took painkillers and muscle relaxants and lay down on the couch, waiting for the pain to go.

Tink didn't have her own cat door but she knew about an unlatched basement window which served the same purpose. Shortly after I lay down, I heard it go *thunk*. Tink pattered up the stairs and jumped on my chest. This was odd. She was *on* me, not curling up at my side.

I pushed her off. But there was something else that didn't go with her. And it moved! I flicked on the light. Blinking up at me, its nose near my chin, was a mouse. Alive.

I shrieked. I'm not afraid of mice but I'd never had one quite this close before. I picked it up and put it outside. Tink followed, a little unwillingly. I shut the door and cautiously lowered myself back down on the couch, my pulled muscles all the while screaming with pain.

About 15 minutes later the basement window thumped again. Tink trotted up the stairs and jumped up once more, dropping the stunned mouse on my chest.

I caught it and put it outside once more, Tink following at my firm request. I lay back down, pain receding. I sighed gratefully. The painkillers were finally kicking in.

Two minutes later, the window thudded again.

Tink had barely landed, mouse in mouth, before I leaped to my feet. The mouse went out the door, followed by a persistent cat muttering a few things about humans not recognising a good thing when they had it. Or that's what I imagined she was saying. She was never one to mince words.

This time I quickly hobbled downstairs to lock the basement window.

As I lay back down on the couch, though, I noticed the agony in my back had faded. I tentatively twisted my shoulder. Definitely much less. I could move it easily; the pain was a weak memory. All my leaping about had worked where medication hadn't.

Apparently Tink was right. A live mouse is the best medicine for what ails you.

Sharman Horwood
Seoul
South Korea

Write to me ... ✉
email Sharman
sharmanh2004@yahoo.ca

Sharman Horwood is a Canadian writer living in Seoul, South Korea.

How can I stop my cat chewing my chin?

Help! My five-month-old female cat Flossy chews on my cheek and chin with her needle-like teeth in the early hours of the morning when I am asleep in bed. My face is much the worse for wear and is causing embarrassing remarks from people. Will the little monster grow out of this habit? None of my other cats ever used their teeth this way.

Can you offer any advice? Contact us at SMARTER than JACK.

4

Smart cats find solutions and learn fast

Time to disconnect

My cat Horatio is a 16-year-old cream point Siamese, and one of the smartest things he has done is cut my phone calls short.

Radio stations in Saskatchewan used to have a lot of contests. I would call in from my kitchen wall telephone, which didn't have a redial function. I'd punch in the number with my right hand, then, if it was busy, quickly press to disconnect with my left hand and then dial again.

Horatio decides how long a phone call should be

Horatio would sit on the dishwasher (which is under the phone) and watch me do this. He saw me click off and redial over and over again. Either I would get through to the station or not, then I would hang up the phone. In his kitty mind he figured out that, if the button was pressed down, eventually I would hang up the phone and pay him some attention. So now if I am on the telephone too long he will reach up with his little paw and disconnect me. He has done this quite a few times and it is very embarrassing to have to call the person back and explain. I guess he figures when I'm home all the attention should be given to him!

Sharon Anne Serbin
Regina, Saskatchewan
Canada

Write to me ... ✉
Sharon Serbin
68 Carmichael Road
Regina SK S4R 0C5
Canada

A cat with ingenuity

One summer day I was changing the cats' litter box. As I usually do, I swept up all the litter gravel that got splashed around the plastic box that I keep in the bathroom, put it in with the stuff in the litter box, emptied the contents into a garbage bag and took the emptied box outside to hose it down.

Imagine my surprise when I went to put it back in the bathroom. On the floor where the box sat was a perfect miniature pyramid of litter box gravel. One of my three ladies had assembled it from gravel on the floor and had obviously used it to make a temporary locale for her pit stop. I'll never know who did it.

Israel Lachovsky
Calgary, Alberta
Canada

Write to me ... ✉
Israel Lachovsky
1314 10 Avenue SE
Calgary AB T2G 0W9
Canada

Zane's game

A short time ago I purchased a 'Busy Box' to keep my cats occupied and amused. It worked and they all seemed to enjoy it.

One day I was watching them play and noticed that all the toys had been batted out of the box. Zane (an eight-month-old kitten) proceeded to go around the room collecting the toys and carrying them back to put them in the holes of the Busy Box. Then they all continued with their game.

Sharon Irwin
Talala, Oklahoma
United States

Write to me ... ✉

Sharon Irwin
7991 S 4060 Rd
Talala OK 74080
USA

Zane plays with the Busy Box

Minou tinkles the ivories

I answered an ad in my local paper for a 'beautiful kitten'. Our dignified ginger tom Becket had died some months previously, and Swish – also ginger but long-haired and, we'd discovered, female – was lonely. Or so we thought.

In fact Minou, our eight-week-old bundle of fun, proved to be less of a companion and more of a thorn in Swish's side. My husband also found her a bit of a bully but I was smitten. She preferred my lap to anyone else's. It had nothing to do with the fact that I fed her – how could you think that? I was happy, anyway; cupboard love is still love.

She chose her own name. A French friend had come to lunch. The kitten was nowhere to be seen and we all went round going, 'Kitty, kitty.' All except Claude, who naturally enough called out, '*Minou, minou.*' Out she came.

She taught herself to open doors as soon as she was big enough. She was good at getting into cupboards too. She discovered that lying on my head was a good way to let me know she was ready for breakfast. She was more than usually fond of her food, was Minou, so I knew she'd be easy to train.

Train a cat? Absolutely. Dogs may be more eager to please and therefore quicker to learn, but cats aren't stupid and often make willing students. Especially the greedy ones. I've trained all my cats to perform simple tricks such as sitting up and shaking hands, and each has seemed happy to oblige.

Almost as important as a clever subject or trainer is an effective training technique, and this is where the 'clicker' comes in. This little gizmo makes a short clear click, and when followed by a treat it soon becomes a reward in itself. Naturally you don't get the final trick immediately, but small movements in the right direction earn a click and a treat so that bit by bit you get what you want.

Getting Minou to shake hands was easy; I just touched her paw, saying 'Shake' at the same time, and waited for her to move it. *Click!* My moving her paw would have been no good; all she'd have learned for her reward would have been to let me do it.

Since Minou was a willing pupil, I decided to train her to play the piano. Believe it or not, it took me only around five sessions of five minutes each to get her to Grade 1. It helped that she already shook hands, because in frustration when first sitting on the bench beside me she offered her paw. I clicked and fed, but only clicked thereafter when her paw got a tiny bit closer to the piano. Soon she was touching the keys and, not long after, pushing them down. Boy, did she get a big treat the first time she made a sound! From then on, I waited until she played a few notes in a row before clicking and giving her a treat.

Her first public performance was on Christmas Day. We had about eight friends there, only one of whom, besides my husband, knew about my musical moggie. Between cheese and dessert I called the table to attention.

'Many of you will know that I've been taking piano lessons,' I began, 'so I thought you might like a little recital.' I got the expected reaction – a stifled groan along with an effort to look pleased – and made my way to the piano. Minou was soon beside me, banging away, up and down the keyboard, before I'd even settled into my accompaniment. She performed magnificently and everyone was duly delighted.

A notice in the *Radio Times* some weeks later asked readers to write to the BBC about their clever pets. I sent in a video of Minou and naturally she was chosen to take part in *Animal Antics*, alas not shown in this country. But *Test Your Pet* with Rolf Harris and Kate Humble was to be shown on BBC 1. Minou's big chance at stardom had arrived.

The researchers had found out about my piano-playing cat, and again we were filmed for telly. It was hard work but worth it, and on the big day family and friends joined us to watch my celebrity cat do her stuff. She sat beside me during the screening, and I don't think I was imagining the look of proud satisfaction on her face as she watched herself banging away at the keys and winning the nation's hearts.

Clever? Of course. The clicker system might deserve some credit, but Minou well deserved her round of applause.

What did she play? I would tell people she preferred to improvise rather than read music and that her style was modern eclectic. No cat, no matter how clever or entertaining, will ever replace her.

Deborah Buzan
London
England

Write to me ... ✉

email Deborah
skizan@blueyonder.co.uk

Jingle bells

His Nibbs, an 11-and-a-half-year-old male Siamese mix, and Ms Riley, a four-year-old female Maine Coon, are housebound kitties living in a small cottage with Moms and Jon. The sign on the door says it all: 'Two spoiled cats live here.' It should say 'Two very smart cats live here'.

The pair have learned – and react properly to – many word commands, including 'What do you want, show me', 'It's not time, just a minute' and now 'Ring the bell'.

Until six months ago, the only contact with the outside world for these smarties was a kitty door cut through the front of the house leading to a secured pen on the front deck. There they could view the beach, with the pelicans, seagulls and many assorted birds using the bird feeder nearby. There were also two individual windowsill perches located at the back of the house, where they lounged, basking in the morning sun and enjoying the cool breezes, while checking out occasional visitors – both human and animal – to Moms's garden. Never satisfied, these two hung out near every outside entry door, trained not to run out but hoping to get a peak at, or smell of, the unknown beyond.

After kitty-proofing the narrow walkway just below the garden which is outside the bathroom door, the pair were at last allowed to wander outside at will. When the door was left open for their convenience they wandered in and out, but so did the flies and bugs.

Moms then taught the pair to ring two large jingle bells that were tied to the doorknob. Though no food rewards were given, they learned they could have their way by stretching up the door and pawing the bells, sending anyone within earshot running to the back door. Usually, one or both cats would sit at the door waiting for someone to arrive. When told to ring the bell they would repeat their act and receive a lot of stroking and the door would be opened for them. This act was cute at first, but it soon got pretty tedious for the humans to appear on command (who was training whom?). So now the bells are attached to the door only when it's convenient for the humans.

Old commands soon became useful to them for their new trick. Upon pestering the humans and hearing 'What do you want, show me', they would run to the back door and sit and wait to see if the bells would magically appear. (They still go through this routine daily, usually in the morning and evening, but if told 'It's not time' they will walk away and try again a short time later.)

Soon after learning the bells trick, they were out back when Moms

49

His Nibbs rings the bell to go outside

had to leave the house. After quickly checking to make sure they were both inside, she closed the door, removed the bells and left the house. When she returned an hour later, His Nibbs began pestering Moms until she finally asked, 'What do you want, show me.' The cat ran to the back door, meowing like crazy. Thinking he just wanted to go out, Moms told him, 'It's not time', but he howled loudly and persisted so she reluctantly placed the bells on the knob. He jumped up and began banging the bells. Concerned, Moms opened the door and in ran a very frightened Ms Riley. Neither cat had ever been out in the kitty run alone and her meows couldn't be heard from inside the house – His Nibbs had rescued Ms Riley.

The humans went on vacation, leaving their regular kitty-sitter in charge of the pair, but forgot to remove the bells. The sitter was told of their new trick, but she apparently didn't take heed of what these two smarties were capable of doing.

While showering early one morning, the sound of jingle bells became louder and louder. At first the sitter was frightened, then bewildered; then, laughing, she peeked out through the shower curtain. Looking up at her were two furry little menaces patiently waiting for their temporary freedom from incarceration.

The moral of this story is, if you are a sitter please pay close attention to what you're told about your intelligent charges. Then, when you think you are the only person in the house, you won't be frightened out of your wits when you hear jingling bells just outside your shower curtain!

Jon and Carol Hammond
San Clemente, California
United States

No toy was safe in that drawer

One day while picking up in the living room I put a couple of cat toys in the drawer of an end table. Later I was working in the kitchen and my then nine-year-old Abyssinian cat Skookum brought in what appeared to be the same toy that I had earlier placed in the drawer, and dropped it at my feet.

I went into the living room and, sure enough, the drawer was open and the toy gone. I put the toy back in the drawer and shut it tightly.

A while later, back came Skookum with the same toy!

After putting the toy back in the drawer I stood back where I could watch him. From his vantage point on the floor he could see under the table and see the drawer move. He walked under the table, reached up and pushed the drawer forward, walked round to the front and proceeded to retrieve his toy.

Although amazing at the time, unfortunately from then on anything ever put in that drawer was fair game for him.

Rene Copeland
Calgary, Alberta
Canada

Tiger the trick-or-treat cat

Tiger was born on my youngest daughter's wedding day. He belonged to my son and, when he and his wife split up, Greg and Tiger came to live with us.

At 6 pm every day, Tiger would sit by the door and wait for Greg to come home from work. I don't know how he knew what time it was but he was there, waiting patiently. When my son eventually moved out, Tiger became ours.

One Halloween night, children were ringing the doorbell to get treats. I heard the doorbell ring about 9 pm and thought it was getting a little late for trick-or-treaters. When I went to the door, there was Tiger, sitting on the ledge and peeking in the door. There were no children in sight.

To this day, he rings the doorbell when he wants to come in. He gets up on the ledge and presses the side of his head against the bell. He gives it one push, but if we take too long getting to the door he continues to push the bell until we answer.

I tutor students after school in my home. Some of the new ones are a little shy and anxious, but Tiger makes them welcome by sitting beside them and letting them pet him. When I am working in the house or yard, Tiger is nearly always at my side. He is a great companion.

Marie Walker
Sutton West, Ontario
Canada

> Write to me ...   ✉
>
> Marie Walker
> PO Box 249
> Sutton West ON L0E 1R0
> Canada

It wasn't the wind

Our cat Poppy has always been slightly 'mental' but more than a bit smart.

Every time I carried her into the kitchen she could see that to open the door I would either push it open or turn the handle. After about a month of this, I was sitting in the kitchen and suddenly heard the door creak open and then shut.

I went to have a look but there was nobody there except Poppy. Assuming it was the wind, I forgot about it. Two days later, I was in the hallway reading when I saw Poppy trotting past. I looked to see

53

where she was going, and saw her walk into the doorway opposite the kitchen door. She took a run-up towards the door, and when she got there she leaped up and shoved the door open.

I never thought my cat was that clever.

Florence Isaacs
London
England

Fang's clever trick

There once was a sleek, smoky grey, yellow-eyed tomcat called Fang. He lived in an old-fashioned house in the seaside town of Lyttelton, New Zealand. On his front door was an old-fashioned door knocker that was very big and old.

When Fang first arrived he was only a kitten, and too small to be outside on his own yet. But as he grew bigger and spent more time outside, Fang learned a very clever trick. After many days – possibly weeks – of watching people come and go, Fang learned that if he used his paws he could use the door knocker to knock on the front door just like the people. When he did this, the door was opened by one of the humans inside – much to their amazement and surprise. Once he learned this trick Fang never looked back. Whenever he needed to get inside, day or night, he would just knock.

This is a true story, and has surprised and made a lot of people laugh, especially when I had to get out of bed to let him in. Fang was a much loved, and now missed, pet.

L Nicholson
Christchurch
New Zealand

Phaedra knows who to wake up

My cat Phaedra is a great huntress. She gets up at 5 am for the best hunting.

Initially, she would run from window to window in our bedroom, causing a ruckus, waking Robert, who would in turn holler loudly and throw her out of the room, defeating her purpose of getting out on the hunting ground at the prime hour.

One day she inadvertently stepped on my radio alarm clock. Gentle classical music, which I have it tuned to, woke me but not Robert, as I have associated the music with waking hour. I got out of bed, half-asleep, stumbled down the stairs and opened the door for her. Penelope, our other cat, followed her out to enjoy some early morning hunting herself.

Clever Phaedra learned how to wake Robin up

Next morning, Phaedra again stepped on the radio alarm clock, turning on the gentle music. The morning after that, she stepped on the radio alarm clock again. I believe this is a pattern. She has figured out how to turn on the alarm to get me up without disturbing Robert, who is not as accommodating as I am, getting her needs met to pursue her vocation as the great huntress.

Robin Wassong
Bellingham, Washington
United States

How can I calm my ragdoll?

I have an 18-month-old ragdoll cat. We found her when she was about three months old and very wild. I have tamed her, but she won't go near my husband or daughter. She will only come to me when she wants to, otherwise I can't get near her either. She won't go outside – she just goes 'mental' if the door is open.

Has anyone got any ideas on how to make her a nice cat and is there anything natural/herbal that we could give her to calm her down?

Can you offer any advice? Contact us at SMARTER than JACK.

Your say . . .

Here at SMARTER than JACK we love reading the mail we receive from people who have been involved with our books. This mail includes letters both from contributors and readers and from the animal welfare charities that have benefited. We thought we would share with you excerpts from some of the letters that really touched our hearts.

'I'd also just like to say I think the work you do to help animals is amazing and I really am delighted to be part of it.'

Diane, England

'Thank you so much for choosing my story! I'm thrilled to bits! I will be telling absolutely everyone to get their hands on this new book. I just love getting my stories each week. Most of them, I must say, bring tears to my eyes! I'm sure your job is very hard, sifting through all the wonderful stories you get sent.'

Samantha, Australia

'I loved the first SMARTER than JACK book and so enjoyed every story.'

Barbara, Canada.

'I thoroughly enjoyed SMARTER than JACK and was thrilled that RSPCA Australia played a part in this groundbreaking book series.'

Dr Hugh Wirth, AM, President, RSPCA Australia

'I just wanted to thank you very much for sending me the second SMARTER than JACK book. As with the first book, I laughed and cried as I read through it and thought it was wonderful! Keep up the good work.'

Nona, Australia

'Thank you – I'm delighted you like the stories. I've been interested in animals all my life, much to my family's chagrin. But then I've never understood when other people don't feel the same way.'

Sharman, Canada

'This is such a good way to make people aware of how there is so much more to animals than we have ever thought. That's why I love your books – happy, sad and astounding stories!'

Betty, Australia

'We have really enjoyed the first book, SMARTER than JACK. I have given seven books away as gifts and they all enjoyed the book.'

Doreen, Canada

'It goes without saying that to create a best-selling series of books about smart animals requires a smart entrepreneur. Jenny Campbell of Avocado Press is just that. From modest beginnings she has, through utter determination and talent, established a successful publishing business with a social conscience. And we are delighted that she chose animal welfare as the benefactor of that conscience.'

Peter Mason, President, Royal New Zealand SPCA

"I feel honoured to be included in such a delightful series of stories."

Joan, New Zealand

'I absolutely loved your first SMARTER than JACK book, and jumped at the chance to purchase the second one as soon as I found out they were available. Although I love reading all the stories, one in particular brought me to tears called "A dog named 'Dog'" about the fishing dog. I totally broke down and sobbed. What a wonderful story. Anyhow, it persuaded me to put fingers to keyboard.'

Pam, Australia

'I totally enjoyed my book and have given them as gifts as well.'

Rose-Ann, Canada

Lisa and Anthea of SMARTER than JACK
enjoy some letters

59

5

Smart cats have fun and outwit others

Fats the dancing cat

Fats was a large, heavy Siamese cat who spent most of his days snoozing in some cosy spot and letting the world go by. But he liked to dance.

Thursday was my dusting day. I hated dusting, so to get myself moving I played loud, lively music on the stereo. When he heard the music, Fats would come running from wherever he happened to be, inside or out.

He leaped straight up from the floor into my arms and laid his head on my shoulder. I would hold his paw as we did our Fred and Ginger numbers.

Eileen Ohrling
North Vancouver, British Columbia
Canada

Note: Fred Astaire and Ginger Rogers were a famous dancing duo who starred in many musicals, including *Top Hat*, *The Gay Divorcee* and *Flying Down to Rio*.

Tiny the Wimbledon cat

Tiny the tennis player

Tiny was a sad little creature when she came to us. Unloved, undernourished and undersized, she would lash out whenever she felt threatened, for her previous owners had mistreated her.

Unlike Ben, our other 'rescue' cat, she had no conception of play. Ben was always ready for a game; the rustle of a paper bag, a piece of string or a tinkle ball would entrance him. Tiny looked as though she wondered what all the fuss was about.

We were throwing a small ball made out of silver paper for Ben, while as usual Tiny watched from her favourite chair. The ball shot past her, and suddenly her paw shot out and she batted it back. Could she do it again? We threw it once more, and this time she caught it in her mouth and dropped it daintily in front of her as if to say, *More?* Needless to say, we obliged. When the match was over, we tucked the ball behind the clock on the mantelshelf in case she might want to play again, but we didn't hold out much hope.

Next morning we found her looking patiently up at the clock. She wouldn't budge until we played tennis again, and she never missed a shot. At last she'd found something that gave her pleasure.

The years have passed, and Tiny is still an enthusiastic tennis player. No longer small (her name is now a bit of a joke), she is plump and loving, and still sits under the clock when she feels in the mood for a match. She's our much loved Wimbledon cat.

Bridget Egan
Broadstairs, Kent
England

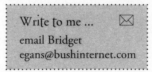
Write to me ...
email Bridget
egans@bushinternet.com

Tell her I want my breakfast

Korky was getting on in years and had gone deaf, which resulted in his meow being a lot louder than it used to be.

We had moved several times and in the latest house we decided against a cat door, due to his propensity for bringing in various forms of wildlife. This meant he shouted at us to be let in or out on demand.

One morning, after a very late night, I was in bed trying to catch up on much needed sleep. Korky was outside, and yelled that he wanted his breakfast – now! I ignored him. He tried again and I turned over and snuggled under the duvet, feeling guilty but not willing to drag myself out of bed.

About three minutes later the doorbell rang. I dragged myself downstairs and opened the door to find my Japanese neighbour in his pyjamas. 'Ah …,' he said, 'Korky, he want in, he come and shout and sing under my window. I open window and say, "What you

63

want?" and he shout at me, then he go to my door. He come back and shout again at me and go to my door, so I go and open door to see what wrong. He take me to your door and look at me, look at bell, look at me, look at bell … so I ring bell for him.'

'Thank you,' I said weakly, aware of Korky's smug expression as he strutted through the doorway.

I of course gave Korky his breakfast and never had the temerity to ignore him again.

Elaine Weir
Crownhill, Milton Keynes
England

Scamp lived up to his name

We had a Siamese cat called Scamp. Throughout his 18 years he caused us much amusement and certainly lived up to his name.

He used to catch rabbits from the nearby fields and bring them home to us, much to our horror. So it was no surprise when, one Sunday morning as I was working in the kitchen, I saw Scamp walking along the top of the fence and carrying what I thought was a rabbit.

When he jumped down onto the lawn, I realised it was actually a whole cooked chicken. I rushed outside, salvaged the chicken from him and took it inside. It was still warm and had obviously been taken out of someone's oven and left on a table to cool. Scamp must have smelt it, carried it off the table and brought it home to us. I felt very guilty about his misdemeanour, but realised I could hardly go round to the neighbours and ask who had lost their Sunday dinner. I never did find out whose it was.

To the rear of our house lived a man on his own, and he and Scamp were great friends. Scamp had a habit of jumping up at door handles, pulling down on them and letting himself in, and this is what he did at the man's house. The man was very pleased for him to do it, but eventually he moved away and another family bought the house.

One night we put Scamp out as usual. We had just gone to bed when a police car and police dog handler arrived at the house behind ours. At this point we saw Scamp making a quick dash over the fence and back to our house. Knowing in our hearts that he was the cause of all the trouble, we hurriedly fetched him in. He had obviously tried to let himself into the house where his friend had lived. The new family, who didn't know him, had seen the door handle move down and thought they had burglars.

Sneaky Scamp was mistaken for a burglar

65

The following day, we asked a few discreet questions as to what the commotion had been about the previous night. The answers proved our assumption to be correct.

Mrs C Goadby
Hinckley, Leicestershire
England

Squeaky investigates some water in his 'laboratory'

An amateur scientist

My husband's cat Squeaky liked to experiment with water. Most cats don't like water except to drink, but he would pick up his bowl and tip it over – just a little at first as the water started to run onto the floor.

66

He would tip the bowl a bit more and a bit more until the bowl was empty and a puddle on the floor. After his water bowl investigation had been performed a few times, they put the bowl in the basement, which led to the second experiment.

My husband's mother used to presoak the laundry in a big sink beside the washer. Squeaky would hook out a piece of wet clothing and let it fall on the floor. He must have found the *splat* quite satisfying, along with watching the water spread on the floor, for he would continue, one piece at a time, until the wash was all on the floor. 'Oh, Squeaky!'

Patricia Grant
Calgary, Alberta
Canada

Oliver was a star

Oliver was a 'free to a good home' kitten when he came to live with us. The result of a one-night stand between a pure-bred Siamese and a local moggie, he developed into an enormous tabby with his mother's cunning and voice.

We planned that our new kitten would sleep in his own comfortable box in the kitchen, with access to all of the house except the bedrooms. Oliver had other ideas. The first night, he scrabbled up the carpet outside our bedroom door. From then on, he slept at the foot of our bed.

It wasn't long before he reigned as boss cat over our neighbourhood. All feline visitors to the garden were promptly dealt with in a flurry of hisses and claws. A pair of nesting blackbirds dropped stones on him in a desperate attempt to keep him away from their fledglings. Oliver had no respect for passing dogs, their human walkers fleeing

67

in a tangle of leads as he hurtled towards them. Nothing seemed to worry a cat who calmly watched thunderstorms and fireworks from the windowsill.

There was just one thing that caused Oliver to seek refuge. As soon as he saw the vacuum cleaner emerging from the cupboard, he fled under the nearest bed. We were able to turn this aversion to our advantage and deter the cat from one of his most annoying activities. Every year, he regarded the Christmas tree as his own

Oliver was a cunning, fun-loving cat

private source of playthings, helping himself daily to baubles, tinsel or other decorations. As the tree was regularly tipped over during these raids, we rapidly lost any feeling of seasonal goodwill towards our pet. We were also worried he might hurt himself.

One of the children hit on a solution. Our Christmas tree gained the extra garland of a vacuum cleaner hose coiled around the base. We hadn't completely spoiled Oliver's fun, as he still managed to release the odd balloon, dribbling it all through the house until it finally burst.

He was a great playmate and became adept at hide-and-seek, jumping out with glee as we pretended to search for him. His favourite game was chasing after a rope dragged around the garden. When we tried to end this exhausting sport by going indoors, we were pursued by a cat letting out a muffled yowl as he carried the end of a rope in his mouth.

I suspect that being a thief of anything edible was part of Oliver's survival instinct. It meant, however, that we dared not leave any food where he could see it. The Christmas turkey had to be defrosted in one of the children's rooms, with a warning notice on the closed door. Oliver knew the turkey was in there, and would sit outside the room for hours, his nose quivering.

We got used to his cunning ways, and even the neighbours avoided carnage by weighting down their dustbin lids. But one morning I was rather perturbed when a lady who lived much further down the road approached me. I wasn't sure how to answer when she asked if we owned a large tabby cat.

Not having sufficient time to lie convincingly, I had to admit that Oliver belonged to us. I was relieved to see a beaming smile as the lady regaled me with tales of how our cat would pay them frequent visits to enjoy a few of his favourite snacks.

'We so much enjoy his company, and he is such a clever cat, isn't he?' she added. 'You'll never guess what he did the other day!'

To be honest, I didn't really want to know. Apparently Oliver's latest party trick had been to open their fridge door when they weren't looking and run off with the remains of the Sunday joint. Fortunately, they saw the funny side of our cat's misdemeanour – but after that, whenever I happened to see this nice lady in the street, I put on a show of being in a great hurry.

When our children left home to go to university, we decided to work abroad. Oliver, now approaching his twilight years, ended his life as the pet of the owners of a cattery where he had spent many holidays. Now he enjoyed the freedom of the grounds, lording it over the visiting cats in their enclosures. We found it amazing that our avid hunter totally ignored the chickens which scuttled around the garden. He obviously knew what would not be acceptable behaviour. He died at the age of 15. Since then we've had several cats, all of them much loved, but Oliver will always have a special place in our hearts. He was a star.

Brenda Worton
Weybourne, Holt, Norfolk
England

Tom's 'health farm'

My late father-in-law Ted Gangell was the caretaker for the Aroona Dam in the far north of South Australia. He owned two pets, a dog called Trixie and a cat he called Tom the Atom Bomb. Tom spent most of his time exploring the bush around the home, while Trixie simply lay in the sun and got fatter and fatter.

Ted decided this wasn't healthy and put Trixie on a diet. She still put on weight so Ted, thinking she must be catching a local rabbit or two, tied her up in the backyard, all to no avail. As she grew to enormous proportions, however, the mystery was solved.

Ted caught Tom sneaking round the back of the house carrying a rabbit in his mouth. Tom placed the rabbit carefully out of sight under the tank stand, arched his back and gave a ferocious cat call. Trixie heard this familiar 'dinner bell' and, moving like a rocket, appeared from nowhere, slid to a halt under the tank and hoed in. No 'cat-chup' was required.

John Watson
Goolwa
South Australia

Write to me ... ✉

email John
quil@iprimus.com.au

Better speak French, the cat's listening

There she was, the puppy my mother wanted, shivering in a shoebox three sizes too large for her. No amount of cuddling could stop her shaking.

My dad suggested putting another animal in with her. A wild cat had birthed her kittens under our porch, so I reached in and pulled out the first one that didn't fight me. That's how we met Cleo and started a 16-year journey with the most interesting cat I ever met.

He figured out how to unlatch the door and let himself out. He pinned corncobs to the floor with all four feet, eating one row at a time. He moved the hose so that he could sleep in dry dirt. He would talk on the phone to my girlfriend but no one else. He'd push his legs against our backs until we were on the edge of the bed and he had all the covers. He didn't like killing mice so he pretended to be scared of them in the house, and then played with them in the garden. But it was years before we discovered how smart he really was.

I'd just cleaned the fishbowl and left it on the counter beside his can of cat food. When Cleo leaped up and found the can still unopened, he swatted one of the goldfish out of the bowl and onto the floor. We were too far away to save the fish before he got to it, so I yelled at him to put the fish back, or else. He ran over to the fish, gently picked it up in his mouth, leaped back up to the bowl, dropped the fish in and ran out the door. We didn't see him again until suppertime.

In spite of the many proofs of his intelligence, our parents refused to believe that the cat understood English so they still discussed cat matters in front of him. That stopped abruptly when Cleo let them in on his secret. Mom was sitting in the living room, complaining bitterly about the cat ruining our supper by chewing through the steak she'd left on the counter to defrost. 'I've had it with that cat,' she said. 'We've got to get rid of it.'

Cleo jumped out of his chair, leaped over my father and onto my mother's lap. He kissed her face and licked her chin until she shook with laughter. It was the first time they had gone near each other since he joined the family. The next time she talked about the cat, she switched to French.

Lyn Dainard
Calgary, Alberta
Canada

Benson outwitted the girls

Benson, my daughter's large ginger tomcat, has a mind of his own.

He found a way to open the fridge and was found one day sitting inside it, having a leisurely wash after pinching some chicken. So my daughter and her friend bought a childproof lock to keep him out.

Benson wasn't to be stopped so easily. One day, after putting some chicken in the fridge to save for sandwich making, one of the girls discovered the fridge was open, the chicken had gone and Benson was again having a wash. Later on, she put some food in the fridge and kept a careful lookout.

When he was sure no one was watching, Benson pushed and banged his head on the door until the lock sprang open. But this time he didn't get the goodies.

Mrs J Reynolds-Warnes
Tydd, Cambridgeshire
England

Tangye is fascinated by water

We named our Manx kitten Tangye after the author Derek Tangye who wrote about some of his cats in the *Minack Chronicles*.

We already had a blue Burmese called Aimee. They take it in turn to chase each other, and Tangye rules over Aimee. He never sleeps; he knocks over bins, the linen basket and the container of cat biscuits. He plays football with Brussels sprouts, and I've found three in the washing machine.

He puts his paws in his water bowl and then washes his face. He likes to sleep in the sink or washing machine, and can't resist a running tap or the water which fills the loo. He even turns on the taps which set off the central heating on our combi-boiler. Having

73

Tangye gets up to all sorts of mischief

turned the radiators on, he basks in the heat. He appears to be left 'handed', by the way.

Once he operated the TV remote control. I went downstairs at 5.30 am, fearing burglars, only to find him watching cartoons.

Yasmin Donlon
Burton-on-Trent, Staffordshire
England

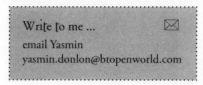

Write to me ...

email Yasmin
yasmin.donlon@btopenworld.com

Fetch, Othello!

In 2000 we were living in Sydney, Australia when we got Othello as a kitten from the Animal Welfare League.

We had lots of fun toys for our lively new kitten to play with. While we expected him to do the usual 'chase the cat toy' and bat it around the room, we got quite a surprise when he started returning the toys to us. His favourite little toy was christened his 'blue thing' and he would play fetch with it almost every day. The blue thing was eventually replaced with a yellow version. The further away it was thrown, the more excited he would get, scampering off after it, collecting it and then racing back to the person who threw it.

In 2002 Othello moved to New Zealand. He continues to play fetch on cue and delights visitors with his antics. I'm still impressed when he trots back to me, toy in mouth, and drops it in my waiting hand for me to throw again.

A Kirk
Wellington
New Zealand

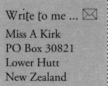

Write to me ...

Miss A Kirk
PO Box 30821
Lower Hutt
New Zealand

75

6

Smart cats make us wonder

A present for Mothering Sunday

It was Mothering Sunday and we had returned home after being out for lunch.

I was relaxing on the settee when my husband said, 'Here's your bouquet coming!' Into the room ran my cat Willow with a large bunch of flowers in her mouth. She jumped up and dropped it in my lap.

She had been in the spare room and must have jumped on the windowsill to get at a large pot of busy Lizzies I had there. I know my husband wouldn't have believed it had he not seen it. She has never done it since, which is probably a good thing because some plants are poisonous to cats.

Mrs J Saunders
Coleford, Gloucestershire
England

Fluffy rose to the challenge

Our black and white moggie Fluffy was a lazy cat who liked to lie in the sun. He didn't enjoy chasing mice and birds.

One summer evening my husband and I sat on a bench in our garden as Fluffy slept on the lawn nearby. I asked my husband if he thought our cat would be able to catch a mouse. He said he thought Fluffy was too fat and lazy.

Well, Fluffy must have been listening because the next morning, when I opened the kitchen blinds, I saw a dead mouse lying on our garden bench.

Perhaps cats understand more of what we say than we think.

Mrs M Farrer
Blackpool, Lancashire
England

How did Marmy know?

For a number of years I was matron of a war veterans' hospital, caring for many old soldiers. Each man had his own room and the atmosphere was as home-like as possible. This of course included having a 'home' cat, Marmalade, who was known as 'Marmy'.

After breakfast each day the men used to sit in the lounge and the subject of conversation was where Marmy had spent the night – that is, whose bed she had slept on. One man who very much kept to himself was all smiles if he had been the one that Marmy chose.

She used to do the rounds but did have a preference for one man in particular. When he became ill and had to go to the hospital, she sat for hours outside his door awaiting his return. Unfortunately, this did not happen as he died in hospital.

As was the case for many of the men, his funeral service was held in the large recreational room at the home with all his old comrades attending.

Everyone was waiting for the service to begin when in walked Marmy. She sat on the floor at the foot of the coffin throughout the service. When the coffin was being carried out to the waiting hearse,

How did Marmy know her special friend had passed away?

Marmy followed right behind with tail erect and waited until the cortège moved off.

How did she know that this was her special friend? She had never done it before that day and never did it afterwards for any other service.

Ngaire Byers
Timaru
New Zealand

Write to me ... ✉

Ngaire Byers
c/- Smarter than Jack
PO Box 27003
Wellington
New Zealand

Her gap year gave her a passion for French fries

Merlot and her brother Bagel were typical inquisitive farm cats who enjoyed the outdoors and exploring far and wide.

Five years ago we moved to the nearby village. Village life was a bit of a shock to the pair, with neighbours, traffic, roads and other cats, as they'd been used to roaming through the open countryside. We kept them in the house for a while, and by spring had still not got a new cat flap fitted.

Over Easter weekend we left the back door ajar so they could come and go. Late on Saturday evening, Merlot was nowhere to be seen. We stayed up most of the night with the back door open.

We plastered the local area with posters and kept an eye on our old house in case she had gone back there. During the following summer I would wander along the paths between the fields, bashing a tin of cat food with a fork and calling out for her. As autumn came, we hoped the dark days would entice her back but she didn't appear.

In the meantime, Bagel gradually got used to the house and we put in a new cat flap.

Eventually I accepted that Merlot had gone for good. In March we went to visit friends in Holland and left Bagel in safe hands. We got back late and went straight to bed. In the middle of the night, the light went on and Jon called me from downstairs. He'd been woken by a second cat jumping on the bed and assumed it was one of the neighbourhood cats bold enough to come in, but was surprised as Bagel had not complained about the feline intruder.

At the foot of the stairs was Merlot, meowing as if nothing had happened. Apart from a fresh cut on her back leg, she appeared to be fine and acted as if she had never been away.

Merlot was away for nearly a whole year. She was not the most sociable of cats and I doubt she would have been taken in by another family. I suspect that, as she was always getting into boxes and even our car, and with a lorry weighbridge nearby, she got herself transported somewhere and spent the year finding her way back. What is remarkable is that she came back to the new house, where she had lived only three or four months, and she came back through the new cat flap.

She has settled down well, is a lot more appreciative of home comforts and purrs a lot more. She still likes to spend the day exploring but always comes home. The only lingering reminder of her 'gap year' is her unexplained new passion for French fries, a taste she must have developed while scavenging on the road.

Janice Broadstock
Faversham, Kent
England

Charlie seems to understand what Pat says

Charlie understands me

When I adopted my Birman cat Charlie Cuddles, he had been found wandering and his owners couldn't be traced. My instinct was to lock him in the house to keep him safe but I was warned that this would make him unhappy. When I gave in and let him out, he set off to explore the neighbourhood, staying out from breakfast time until teatime. One day I could take no more.

Before I opened the door, I looked him in the eye and said firmly, 'You can go out but please stay where I can see you. It worries me when I don't know where you are.'

Off he went, did a tour of the front lawn and then settled under the hedge, not leaving the garden all day. When he came back in, I thanked him for staying in the garden – it's only polite, after all.

From then on, I have said simply, 'Stay where I can see you', and he does. It's so reassuring.

Charlie also has a good understanding of my routine. The doctor advised me to listen to a relaxation tape for half an hour each day to help bring down my stress levels, and Charlie recognises the signs of preparation.

Tape player and headphones go on, I stretch out on the settee, my eyes closed, and Charlie instantly joins me. He stretches out on my chest, one paw each side of my neck, and closes his eyes. As I practise my slow deep breathing, he practises his slow deep purring. It's as therapeutic as the tape. It may be that he just likes to lie on a warm body but I prefer to think that he too is benefiting from the relaxation tape.

I believe all my 'rescue' cats can pick up on my thoughts. They'll be on my bed, and I'll be downstairs watching TV and think to myself, 'Right, I'll feed the cats next.' Before I can move, there are four thumps from upstairs as they all jump off the bed and come running for their food. I never have to call them. We have a real connection – it's so lovely.

Pat James
Rugeley, Staffordshire
England

Ma returned with a surprise for me

When my brother left Calgary for another province about 20 years ago, I agreed to take his cat Ma. I was moving into a new basement apartment in Calgary.

On moving day we put Ma in the bathroom of the new apartment, with the door shut to keep her from escaping while we were busy toing

83

and froing and moving things in. Unfortunately the unthinkable happened and someone opened the bathroom door. Ma was gone in a flash.

We searched high and low for weeks but couldn't find her. But one evening two months later we were in the apartment and saw a cat at the window. It was Ma, and she had a newborn kitten in her mouth.

When I opened the window she brought the kitten in to show me. I got a box and made a nice warm place for them both. I left the window open and waited to see if she would bring more babies but she didn't.

It still amazes me that this little cat would bring her new kitten to the one safe place she remembered, even though she had previously spent less than four hours there.

L Sparrow
Okotoks, Alberta
Canada

Tabby predicts seizures

Our cat Tabby has proved to be a predictor of my son's seizures.

He usually has seizures at night. Tabby often sleeps with him, but if you happen to notice that she is actually sleeping on top of him, it is almost a guarantee that he will have a seizure that night. We take great notice of where Tabby sleeps.

Tanya Kitchen
Fredericton, New Brunswick
Canada

Domino the telephone operator

Answer the phone, please

Domino was four or five weeks old when she came into my life.

I was living temporarily at a friend's house in London. One sunny afternoon some children from the other end of the street arrived and gave my friend a kitten. My friend was on the phone at the time and didn't realise she'd consented to having a kitten, but there it was.

A few days later, the kitten became poorly and a trip to the vet was necessary. This duty fell to me, as my friend and her family had decided to go on holiday. It soon became apparent that the kitten was not wanted, and as I'd become attached to her I had to find a place for her and myself.

During her illness I took her to work in a cat basket lined with a hot-water bottle. I made sure she had her medicine, and fed her fluids with a syringe when she couldn't eat. Against all the odds she pulled through, and we moved into a tiny bedsit. I called her Domino as she was black and white.

Once she'd recovered, I left her at home when I went to work, and she was always waiting for me when I returned. One thing I did notice, though, was that the telephone was often off the hook. The phone, which was bright green, was kept on the floor and I assumed Domino knocked the receiver off when she was playing.

I noticed that whenever the phone rang she came running towards it, so I asked my sister to ring me and just let it keep ringing. Sure enough, Domino ran over and removed the receiver with her paw.

I never did understand why she did this. Maybe the sound of the ringing attracted her, or perhaps she disliked the sound and wanted to stop it.

A few months later I moved back north and took Domino with me. Although the new phone never held quite the same attraction for her, occasionally she'd jump up onto the telephone table when it rang.

Judith Coulson
Whitley Bay, Tyne and Wear
England

Write to me ...   ✉

email Judith
judescc@yahoo.co.uk

Walks aren't the same without Sophie

It was Sophie's loud howl that got our attention. She lived over the road but because she didn't get on with her two kittens – now grown up – her owner said we could keep her.

She quickly solved our mouse problem. And what a faithful cat she turned out to be, just like a dog in some ways. She liked to keep watch in front of the house, and if we went out for a walk she would come too.

In those days we lived by a bridle path which crossed the Stratford-upon-Avon canal. We loved to go for family walks along the canal towpath. Our dog Ruthy had always come with us but had recently died of old age.

Sophie would simply appear through the hedge, after crossing two gardens, and insist on coming with us. It was as though she knew we missed our faithful dog. As we went along the towpath, which was in a cutting near where we lived, Sophie would walk along the bank, thus avoiding any strange dogs. If we were on level ground, she would pop through the hedge into the adjoining field and wait there until the dog and its owner had passed.

We never took Sophie further than where the railway line crossed the canal. She didn't like the hourly trains so we would leave her in a wooded area just before the railway line. We continued our walk along the canal, usually going as far as the aqueduct and coming back along the same route. Sophie always waited, greeting us with her loud howl.

Occasionally we'd come back by a different route. Sophie waited where we had left her – sometimes until well after dark, if we forgot her, even though she knew the way home perfectly well. I would have to go back with a torch, feeling bad about leaving her for so long. But when I called her, she always responded with a loud howl and followed me home.

She would get very hot during summer walks; three miles an hour is quite a fast speed in a fur coat. On arriving home, she liked to lie on the cold kitchen floor to cool off.

Then we moved to another house, with no bridle path nearby. Sophie would still follow us if we let her, but it's too dangerous on the roads. A walk just wasn't the same without her.

But Sophie was not to be outdone. Five months back, we got a new puppy called Poppy. At first, Sophie looked askance at her. Then

the other night when I was walking Poppy up to the golf course – a short walk that didn't involve crossing the road – Sophie decided to come too. Sophie often walks up to the golf course with us now.

Peter Griffiths
Solihull, West Midlands
England

A feline Antarctic hero

Mrs Chippy still manages to give dogs a fright – even though he's been dead since 1915.

The famous tabby cat from Ernest Shackleton's 1914–17 Antarctic expedition was remembered in 2004 with a life-size statue, commissioned by the New Zealand Antarctic Society. It was placed on the New Zealand grave of the ship's Scottish carpenter, Harry McNeish, who never forgave Shackleton for ordering his beloved cat to be shot.

Scottish friends apparently gave Harry the cat, and it's said that Harry found him curled up in one of his toolboxes as though determined to go on the *Endurance* along with the crew. Shackleton wouldn't have objected, for a good mouser was a valued crew member, with so many rats and mice on board.

In Britain a 'chippy' is an informal term for a carpenter, and Mrs Chippy followed Harry around like a possessive wife. The name stuck even when he was found to be a tomcat, and diary entries show that the crew liked to think of him as female. Apparently he would prowl round on top of the sledge dogs' kennels, enraging them by sharpening his claws on the wood and calmly washing himself just out of their reach. He became a special friend of the young Welsh crewman Percy Blackborrow, who had stowed away in Buenos Aires;

and the only known photograph of the cat, taken by the Australian photographer Frank Hurley, shows him perched on Percy's shoulder. He climbed the ship's rigging like 'a seaman going aloft', according to Captain Frank Worsley.

One ominous night, Mrs Chippy jumped through a porthole into the freezing cold South Atlantic ocean. The officer of the watch heard his cries and actually turned the ship around to pick him up with a net. He soon recovered.

In January 1915 the *Endurance* became trapped in frozen ice. Mrs Chippy disappeared for five days and the crew were distraught. He turned up again and was doubtless given extra treats. But after a month or so it was obvious the ship wasn't going to move, and the dogs were moved off the deck into 'kennels' made from blocks of ice on the ice floe beside the ship. It seems the bo'sun accused Mrs Chippy of teasing the dogs and threatened to throw him to them, but Percy Blackborrow managed to save his life. Others must have shared Percy's love for the cat, as a formal complaint was made against the bo'sun and he was demoted.

Mrs Chippy was weighed at some stage, and unlike the human crew he was heavier than when he'd started the voyage, so a diet of seal meat and pemmican must have agreed with him.

By October the *Endurance* was breaking up under the pressure of ice. A crew member said later that Mrs Chippy spent most of his time sleeping, and his 'almost total disregard for the diabolical forces at work on the ship was more than remarkable – it was inspirational'.

Eventually they all had to camp out in tents on the ice. Shackleton decided to head for the nearest land, hundreds of miles away, and the men could take only what was absolutely essential. That meant that Mrs Chippy, along with the dogs and puppies, would be shot.

Harry McNeish's diary – held by the Alexander Turnbull Library in Wellington, New Zealand – has the following entry for Sunday,

89

November 28, 1915: 'We got three seals today. I am not working today as I feel a bit off with my old trouble the piles. They have been exercising the dogs round the floe. I expect we will have to part with the dogs one of these days as we can't take them with us in the boats. It will be a sad day as we all have taken to the dogs. I had to part with my Missis Chippie the day after we left the ship. I was hurt but I knew it was impossible to take her with us.'

This seems a stoical reaction but the loss must have rankled. It was Harry McNeish who refitted the *James Caird*, the lifeboat which eventually set out for South Georgia Island, and his workmanship played a big part in saving the men's lives. Yet Shackleton refused to recommend him for a Polar Medal, which outraged those who knew the contribution he'd made.

Harry McNeish later returned to his family in Scotland, but must have been restless as in 1925 he emigrated to New Zealand. He was unable to work, with permanently aching hands, and spent his last years living rough on the Wellington docks, supported by wharfies (dock labourers) who considered him a hero. He died in 1930 and was given a naval funeral, but his grave was unmarked until the New Zealand Antarctic Society erected a headstone in 1957.

In 2004 he was 'reunited' with his cat. A life-size bronze statue of Mrs Chippy, the work of Chris Elliot of Hawkes Bay, was placed at the end of his grave in the old Karori cemetery, Wellington. Among those present at the unveiling was Harry's 76-year-old grandson, Tom McNeish of Scotland, who said he believed the cat was more important to his grandfather than the Polar Medal. Baden Norris, curator of Antarctic history at the Canterbury Museum, met Harry McNeish as a child. He said the only thing he ever remembered him saying was that Shackleton had shot his cat.

In recent years Mrs Chippy has been the subject of a book, *Mrs Chippy's Last Expedition*, by Caroline Alexander, and appeared in a film, *Shackleton*, where he was played by a cat named Mac.

Mrs Chippy continues to 'keep watch' from Harry's grave, and still manages to get dogs worked up. I'm told that dogs visiting Karori cemetery do a double take when they catch sight of the statue, convinced that it's a real live cat.

Patricia Reesby
Wellington
New Zealand

Write to me ... ✉
email Patricia
reesby@actrix.co.nz

An obedient patient

Our 11-year-old diabetic cat Felix must have insulin injections twice daily.

He presents himself at the correct times – 9 am and 9 pm – without any prompting, even getting himself into the correct position.

He also watches birds quite benevolently, and never tries to catch them. One day during summer he was lying on the lawn twitching his tail when a magpie flew down and walked all round him.

The magpie pecked his tail not once but twice before flying off. It left an indignant and bewildered cat licking his mental wounds.

Kathleen Martin
Acton, London
England

Do they know when the rain is coming?

Is there any scientific evidence that animals know when rain is coming?

Two of our cats have displayed totally different behaviour before heavy rain.

From a very early age, our grey tabby Benny would simply refuse to go outside on some mornings. At times it was brilliantly fine and sunny, yet he would sit before the open door and refuse to budge. We soon realised that he was never wrong and he became our resident forecaster.

Our tortoiseshell Jasmine had another trick that we took a little longer to recognise. When little more than a kitten, she would struggle through the cat door with a cast-off part of a cabbage tree, that was longer than she was, in her mouth. She would sometimes play with it, but she always left it in a part of the house where everyone could see it. We thought it was a game for her, but after a while it became obvious that she did this only before particularly heavy rain.

Nothing about animals' intelligence surprises us and we are interested to know how common this ability is.

Can you offer any advice? Contact us at SMARTER than JACK.

7

Smart cats prevent disasters

Mission accomplished

Rascal was a slim kitty with shiny black fur and beautiful gold eyes. His favourite food was a juicy ripe persimmon. When he was small he spent the day with me, riding on my forearm between home and our rural hardware store next door. In the station wagon, he rode in back with one claw fastened in the carpet.

One day he jumped up on my desk in the store and wouldn't settle down for his usual nap. He kept bothering me so that I couldn't work. Finally I stood up and he headed for the door. I followed, let him out and closed the glass door again as he started down the steps. Immediately, Rascal returned to the door.

Doris, our clerk, said, 'That's odd. I just let him in. Maybe he wants you to follow him.' I opened the door, and Rascal headed down the steps and walked briskly down the path to our house, leading me to the 'people' door rather than his own.

Inside, the chimney to our wood stove had separated and the house was filling with smoke. I reached down to pat his head and say thank you, and Rascal trotted off down the yard about his own business, his mission accomplished.

Mary Ann Rais
Redding, California
United States

Write to me ... ✉
email Mary Ann
maryrais@yahoo.com

93

Colombus the smoke detector

We'd been out, but had a feeling that we needed to go home. Once there, my husband and I tried to read but couldn't concentrate.

Colombus, our black and white cat, kept crying and running to the furnace room of our apartment. We could find nothing wrong. Finally we got down on the floor, where we saw wisps of smoke curling up through a hole in the floor.

We called the fire department. Firefighters had to break open the door of the apartment downstairs. They found a chair smouldering and the apartment full of smoke. The tenant had been overcome by smoke inhalation.

The firefighters said later that the whole apartment had been about to go up in flames. If we had not followed our wonderful smoke detector Colombus, the outcome may have been tragic.

Patricia Grant
Calgary, Alberta
Canada

Ling's nagging may have saved their lives

Ling, my grandparents' cat, is Tonkinese – a mixture of Siamese and Burmese.

He's 16 now and suffers from arthritis, kidney failure and glaucoma, but still loves life. He's a terrible nag, and even though he is supposed to be on a low protein diet he nags my grandma so much that she often gives in and he gets tuna fish and chicken. But this talent for nagging saved my grandparents' house from being robbed. He may even have saved their lives.

It was six years ago, in February. My grandparents had gone out to rent a video, and when they returned they forgot to turn on the

Ling's meowing saved the day

alarm. They went to the family room at the back of the house to watch their movie, unaware that the robbers were watching them and had parked their van in the neighbours' dark driveway. The neighbours were away from home.

Stealthily the burglars began to break in to the front of the house, where family heirlooms and antique furniture were kept. Little did they know that a pair of green eyes was watching them from beneath a bush. Even if they had known, they probably wouldn't have paid much attention to a small brown cat.

Ling jumped up on the roof, went inside through the bathroom window and ran down to my grandparents in the family room. He was agitated and meowed frantically. He kept running to the door as if he wanted my grandma to follow him.

My grandma reluctantly left the warm room and followed him. Ling started jumping at the dining room door handle. 'Ling, what do you want to go in there for? It's far too cold,' my grandpa said, but Ling kept nagging. Finally my grandpa turned the key and opened the door. To his horror, two men were carrying the family furniture out to the waiting van.

My grandpa ran to the phone and called the police. When they arrived, they said that if Ling hadn't disturbed the robbers they would have stolen everything in that room and possibly even attacked my grandparents. The robbers did get some stuff but Ling saved most of it.

Ling is mellow, loving and affectionate and we all love him. He looks so wise, as if he knows everything.

Sarah Morel
Greystones, County Wicklow
Ireland

Anyone for toast?

A friend of mine, Nat, takes in stray cats and sends them to a local vet for a check-up before releasing them in his spacious backyard.

Occasionally the odd stray hangs around indoors and keeps Nat company. Muska was one such tabby, and Nat was only too happy to accept the stranger into his home.

Within a week, Muska had demonstrated his keen observation. He learned to open all the doors by jumping up and clutching the handle with his forepaws and allowing gravity to do the rest. Nat was also convinced that Muska was destined for an operatic career, since he would imitate his voice in a range of different pitches. All Nat had to do was speak in high and low tones and Muska would respond by meowing in a similar tone.

The most startling of Muska's talents showed itself one hazy Wellington morning. At the time, Nat had a flatmate who used their toaster in the morning while Nat was still in bed.

Of course, when overworked, toasters go on strike and that morning was such a time. Two slices of white bread were in the appliance, well on their way to becoming toast, but they failed to pop up. Nat's flatmate forgot about them and, in his haste to get to work, left the house. The flames surfed the air above, onto an overhead light fitting.

Nat was woken by Muska clawing at his shirt. The cat leaped off the bed and meowed for his companion to follow him. Nat tackled the blaze while Muska took refuge under his bed, resurfacing only when he was convinced that Nat had addressed the problem to his satisfaction.

Ed N Abdool
Wellington
New Zealand

97

That overblanket wasn't safe at all

Susie was the family cat for 19 years. A common black moggie with a few flecks of white on her chest, she formed a special bond with my father.

There were several places she liked to sleep, and one was on Dad's bed, where she would curl up beside his feet. One cold winter's night, my parents were using a supposedly safe electric overblanket to keep warm. Dad was fast asleep when he was suddenly woken by Susie scrabbling at the sheets around his face. Glancing down, he was greeted by the sight of flames. A fault in the electric blanket had caused an acrylic sheet to catch fire.

The shouting woke my brother Mike, who grabbed the sheets and blankets and threw them out of the window. Meanwhile, Susie bolted downstairs and out the cat flap.

To this day, Dad maintains that Susie woke him deliberately and, in doing so, prevented the situation becoming much more serious. She was a clever cat in other respects too. She learned to associate doors and keys, and would sometimes jangle the keys that hung on the kitchen wall when she wanted to go out.

David Tipping
Harrogate, North Yorkshire
England

Sissy saved her brother

I have two grey cats, brother and sister, named Buddy and Sissy.

One day I opened the door to Sissy, who was desperately trying to get my attention. I said, 'Sis, what's the matter, what's wrong?' She walked downstairs and turned at the foot of the stairs to see if I was following.

I obeyed, and as I turned the corner I saw Buddy with his flea collar caught between his upper and lower jaw, trying with all his might to unhook it out of his mouth. He had blood all over his paws and face. I picked him up and ran to the kitchen for a pair of scissors to cut the collar off his neck.

I carried him to the bathroom to clean up the blood and see how much damage had been done. All the while, Sissy was at my side, watching what I was doing. If it wasn't for her smart thinking I doubt if I would have saved Buddy in time. He may have choked to death and I would never have known until it was too late.

Joanne Kelly-Cook
Newfoundland
Canada

A smoke detector named Felix

Felix was a cute tortoiseshell kitten who became depressed after her friend Nala was run over. She wouldn't jump up to the window in the back door when we left, or rush about as usual.

My older brother Christopher had friends over for his thirteenth birthday and didn't want us around, so my mum took my brother and me to town. We were there for two hours.

It seems Christopher left chips in the pan and they caught fire. Felix smelt the fire and managed to jump one of those gates which are supposed to stop babies. Somehow she opened a door and ran up the steps to the upstairs corridor. One way or another, she knew which room Christopher was in. She scratched on his door, hissing.

Chris opened the door and Felix ran round in circles, meowing. By that time, the fire was so bad the smoke was seeping into my brother's room. Everyone ran out of the house, and Chris made it his priority to look after the heroine who had saved his life. He passed Felix to a friend and went back inside to phone the fire brigade. By this time the tiles on our roof had turned black.

Felix is probably better than a smoke alarm, though I don't advise it.

Yasmin Sara Dadkhah
Winchester, Hampshire
England

Sandy pressed the alarm

Most people think cats aren't intelligent, but they have never had a cat like Sandy, my pale ginger tomcat.

I am disabled and have a problem walking. I was fast asleep one night, and in the very early hours of the morning I was woken by the sound of my alarm going off.

Sandy had set it off, and I believe he'd done so deliberately. When I lifted my head off the pillow, I could smell smoke. I managed to get out of bed and look around but everything was safe. The smoke I could smell was wood burning on the allotments opposite my bungalow.

Since then, Sandy presses the alarm when he wants to go out in the middle of the night.

Susan Whale
Mansfield, Nottinghamshire
England

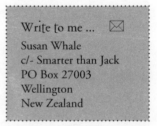

Write to me ... ✉
Susan Whale
c/- Smarter than Jack
PO Box 27003
Wellington
New Zealand

Sandy alerted Susan to danger by setting off the alarm

Come on, wake up!

I became one of countless victims who have had the misfortune to be burgled during the dead of night while sleeping. I'm pleased to say that my story has a much happier ending than most.

The thief only managed to get away with a couple of mobile phones that were on charge on the kitchen worktop. The reason? When the thief entered the lounge from the kitchen, my cat Felix ran swiftly past him and up the stairs into my bedroom, where he launched himself onto my chest and began to meow loudly in my face.

He is a huge black and white tomcat so the sheer weight on my chest was enough to wake me. I pushed him onto the floor, which made a loud thud. He was persistent and jumped straight back, his meows getting louder and more frantic by the second. It was then

101

I realised something was wrong. I usually shut Felix and his mum Sophie in the kitchen when I go to bed, as they have a habit of prowling and annoying my elderly dog Sam, who likes his sleep.

I made my way reluctantly downstairs. In retrospect, this was probably a silly thing to do but someone had to see what all the fuss was about. When I entered the kitchen I found the back door wide open. I knew I hadn't left it open. I may be 50 and a bit forgetful, but not locking the back door wasn't an option.

It was then I knew I had been burgled. The sound of Felix meowing and my grumpy voice shouting at him must have scared the thief away, or perhaps it was the sight of a large cat lunging up the stairs that was the scary part. Whatever the reason, he went without the video, stereo and other large items he'd left in a pile by the kitchen door. His only spoils were the mobile phones.

The bizarre thing is: as I mentioned earlier, I have a dog and he will bark at anything and anyone. Guess what? Yep, that's right, he slept through the whole incident, only crawling out of his bed to see what all the fuss was about when the police arrived. I can only imagine the conversation between Felix and Sam: *Sam, your job is to guard the home from unwanted intruders and mine is to patrol the garden and protect the flower seeds from hungry birds.*

Sam did walk around with his ears back for the rest of the day, but he was soon his old self again so Felix must have forgiven him. I know I have.

Beverley Holland
Halliwell, Bolton, Lancashire
England

My cat saved my life

Over summer there were many forest fires in our area of Vernon, British Columbia, and the smoke was making it hard for me to breathe. I was in hospital for 14 days because of this.

One night I was sound asleep when my Siamese cat woke my husband by walking up and down his back. I was rushed to hospital and just made it before I choked to death. My cat saved my life and is my best friend.

S Schneider
British Columbia
Canada

One cat's opinion

Her name was Jennie. I thought she was the most beautiful, sweetest, and certainly the smartest cat on the planet – even before she alerted me to danger! Perhaps you can forgive me for this bias when I say that Jennie was my first animal companion, despite the fact that I was in my mid-thirties. I had always wanted a cat but allergies prevented it. I was still allergic to cats when I brought Jennie home from the SPCA … but that's a whole other story!

One of Jennie's most endearing traits was that she talked a lot. She made her observations and opinions known – loudly. For the most part, I enjoyed hearing her commentary, although occasionally I would tell her to keep quiet. She would grumble a bit, then make herself comfortable where she could glare at me.

It was when Jennie was about a year old that she demonstrated – to me at least – her superior intelligence. One cold winter evening I was curled up on the couch watching television. Shortly after I

103

got comfortable, Jennie appeared in the doorway to the TV room, talking in her loudest voice. I invited her to hop up on my lap and told her 'Hush'. She refused both suggestions and began to pace in the doorway. As this was unusual behaviour, I got up and went towards her. As I got closer she would move further down the hall, all the while looking back over her shoulder to make sure I was following her. She continued her non-stop caterwauling.

When it became obvious she was leading me to the kitchen, I thought perhaps her food or water dish was empty – but then I remembered filling both earlier in the evening. Suddenly it hit me – the smell of escaping gas. I dashed the rest of the way into the kitchen while Jennie stood just outside it.

The apartment was very old and the gas stove an antique. The oven actually had to be lit with a match every time I used it, but the burners had a pilot light that was always on. The pilot light had gone out and the kitchen was filled with gas fumes. (Natural gas has no odour, but an artificial odour of rotting apples is added so that people will know when it is leaking.)

I opened the kitchen window, got out of the kitchen and closed the door behind me. I was on the phone to the natural gas emergency line within minutes, and in less than 30 minutes the technician was at the door. He fixed the problem, and after an hour with some windows open the apartment was again a safe place to light a match.

The big question is: was Jennie aware of the danger, or was she just wanting me to do something about the awful smell that was assaulting her sensitive feline nose? Of course there's no way of knowing, but Jennie lived with me for 15 years and during that time demonstrated an astounding ability to solve problems. One thing is certain, though – had she not alerted me to the problem when she did, it could have become a very nasty situation.

104

Jennie died ten years ago and, although I now have three cats, I have never come across another cat as clever or as opinionated as she was. I miss her still.

Lyn O'Keefe
Vancouver, British Columbia
Canada

How can I make my cat respect me more?

My cat Martha has a problem with authority. In Martha's mind, my husband is at the top of the ladder – Martha will do anything he says. I bet she would even go and make him a cup of tea if he asked her to.

Me, however, I'm on the bottom rung! Martha will not do anything I say. For example, if I tell her not to scratch the furniture she will just get all excited and scratch it more. In bed at night she also sits right on my chest by my face. I initially thought it was a sign of affection, but now I feel like she's got me pinned down – she's in control.

Can you offer any advice? Contact us at SMARTER than JACK.

Why do cats scratch like this?

When my cat greets me he does so by stretching out his front legs and scraping the carpet vigorously with his claws. The poor carpet is beginning to look quite scruffy. Every time he does this I tell him, 'DON'T scratch the carpet!' and sometimes I lift his paws to emphasise my point. But cats are not noted for obedience, are they? I've tried laying a spare piece of carpet inside the door for him to use, but no – only the 'real' carpet will do. Friends tell me their feline companions also do this.

Can you offer any advice? Contact us at SMARTER than JACK.

8

Smart cats take possession

A disgruntled cat finds a solution

During the 1970s I had a cat called Henry, a large tabby female named (for reasons I won't go into here) after King Henry VIII.

At the time, I shared a flat in north London with a friend called Nick. We used the kitchen as our communal living area, and apart from wooden dining chairs it contained only one comfortable armchair with cosy cushions.

This chair was next to the oven, which was often left on to heat the room. I don't need to tell you that this was Henry's favourite seat, but Nick rather liked it too.

One evening Nick had settled down to watch our small black and white television, while a rather disgruntled Henry had to sit on the floor. Eventually Henry got up, walked slowly to the door and scratched to go out. No sooner had Nick jumped up to open the door than the devious cat ran behind him and claimed the now vacant (and warm) seat.

We never knew her exact age but Henry lived to be over 20, a wise old cat indeed.

Norma Victor
London
England

Henry got her favourite chair back

Jonty stole toys to play with

My cat Jonty used to provide his own toys.

He's a bit of a loner and has a bad temper, so I have to be one step ahead of him all the time. He attacks me on little provocation, and has given me some nasty scratches and bites. He'll sit on my knee, purring and kneading, but only on his own terms.

One day I heard him come inside through his cat flap. He went into the sitting room and started jumping around and playing with something. I hoped it was not a bird or a mouse – not unheard of. I saw that it was something green, and on closer inspection found it to be a small beany 'alien' toy.

Goodness knows where it came from. I imagined him grabbing it off some poor child in a pushchair, or going into someone's house

108

to pinch it. He played with it for quite a while, until the next toy arrived.

I was hanging out the washing in the back garden when I trod on something soft. It was a small, soft, brown beany dog, one of those given away with a McDonalds meal. Several more were to follow, all brought in through the cat flap. We have a tiny tiger, two giraffes, a seal with a ball on its nose, a puppy, a donkey and even Uncle Bulgaria from the Wombles. Jonty brought them all inside and played happily with them. I never knew where they came from.

I did phone my local radio station to ask if anyone was missing toys but no one responded. After a while he stopped bringing them home, so maybe someone became wise to him and stopped leaving them lying around.

Once he brought a cooked pork chop home, possibly off someone's barbecue. I've also found him in the garden, trying to eat a ham sandwich still wrapped in cling film. He catches birds and mice, and one day I came home to find a dead pigeon behind my sitting room chair – not a nice gift. When my grandchildren visited, if they left a soft toy lying around he would be off with it, hiding behind a chair and toying with it as though it was a mouse. We had many a tussle trying to get it off him.

Mrs M F Jones
Walderslade, Chatham, Kent
England

Hang on to your wine glass

My daughter's cat Roux likes to drink alcohol.

When I first met him I was cautioned to hang on to my wine glass. Roux dips his paw into the wine and then licks it. If he spots a

109

beer bottle on the table he'll tip it over and lap up the contents from the tabletop.

There were several empty – or so we thought – beer bottles on the kitchen floor. I saw him walk over and knock against them. He could tell by the sound which bottle had any liquid left in it, and would knock it over and drink the remains off the kitchen floor.

Since cats shouldn't drink alcohol, we now have to be very careful where we put down our glasses or empty bottles when Roux is around!

Otto Schilling
Saskatoon, Saskatchewan
Canada

Toi-toi the eel catcher

We shared our three-masted Chinese junk with a ginger and white cat for more than 13 years. The land scared him, but there was little he feared about his floating home.

He growled at dogs if their owners rowed too close, and was the scourge of seagulls when their cheeky teasing made them careless. Dolphins and other large sea creatures fascinated him.

We were moored in the Hatea River at Whangarei, New Zealand for a large part of Toi-toi's life and he became an expert fisher, using the dinghy as his platform. With a feline's inherent patience he would perch for long periods on the gunwale, with his nose just millimetres from the water and little more than his tail to keep him from tumbling in.

All of a sudden, with the flick of a paw, his quarry would be scooped into the dinghy. Once, it was a swimmer crab that covered his face in froth as he carried it proudly around the deck. Occasionally a flash

110

Toi-toi enjoyed his catch – a nice tasty eel

of silver announced an imprudent fish, but mostly it was an eel.

Toi-toi was a good swimmer and got himself back in the dinghy if he fell in. We would be blissfully unaware of these unplanned dips until he rubbed his saturated fur against our legs after trailing salt water down below and onto the carpet.

At night, while we slept, our intrepid hunter was often out in the dinghy catching an eel for a late snack. In the morning when we collected his presumably empty bowl, the bloody remains of a slimy eel might await us. His victim – often close to a metre long and 50 millimetres in diameter – would have been dragged up to the boat, into the pilot house and down a steep set of steps, then along the carpet to his eating area forward of the saloon.

Blood would be splattered head high in the pilot house when the battle was fierce and, together with the slimy carpets, presented quite a cleaning job. The last straw was when my departure for work was delayed by the messy task of removing blood and slime from my good shoes.

We began to lock Toi-toi in at night but this did not go down well, so once when we returned from a night out square dancing we softened our stance. 'Okay, just for a minute while we get out of our fancy clothes,' we told him.

Well, a minute was all it took for our talented puss. We had barely begun discarding our finery when a couple of thumps on deck warned us of his success. Yes, a nice tasty eel.

Wendy Willett
Russell Island, Queensland
Australia

Clever Smokey tricked his father out of a comfortable spot

A son outwits his dad

Here's a story for you about my two cats, Tinker (12 years old) and Smokey (11 years old). Tinker is Smokey's father. This is what happened when I brought a large plastic bowl home from my friend's place. I had taken it there to use for chips while we were playing cards. Don't let anyone tell you that animals don't have feelings – this story proves that they do.

When I got home, I put the bowl on the couch and left it there. Smokey soon discovered it and found that it was the right size for him to curl up in, so he did and went to sleep for a while. Then he got out and Tinker got into it. After Tinker had been in it for a while, Smokey decided that he wanted to get back in. But he had

113

to get Tinker out of the bowl first. Smokey acted like he wanted to play with Tinker, so Tinker got out of the bowl to join in. As soon as Tinker got out of the bowl, Smokey climbed in and curled up again. He didn't want to play; he was just pretending, to get Tinker out of the bowl. Is that guy sneaky or what! You should have seen how dejected Tinker looked. He sat on my side of the couch and kept staring at Smokey in the bowl. We could tell that he wanted to get back in the bowl again, but he didn't challenge Smokey. I guess he's not as crafty as Smokey is.

Later on that night, when I was walking into the bedroom, Smokey was in front of me. I called Tinker's name and Smokey looked behind him to see if Tinker was there.

They both gave us a lot of laughs that night.

Bonnie Briggs
Toronto, Ontario
Canada

Write to me ... ✉

Email Bonnie
bonniebriggs@yahoo.ca

Don't leave anything lying around ...

Garfield is a small ginger and white cat who lives in a house above Otaika School in Whangarei.

Every night he goes down to the school and brings home any children's socks he finds lying around the playground. Every morning his owners find two or three socks on their front doormat. He drags them across a paddock and through two fences to take them home.

In summer, when the children aren't wearing socks, he visits the swimming pool in search of other items of clothing. All these he proudly brings home – even knickers. Once he tried to steal a jumper but it got stuck in the wire fence.

Hang on to your socks . . . Garfield's on the prowl!

The schoolchildren are warned that, if they leave things lying around, Garfield will get them. He even takes the neighbours' socks if they're left outside.

Every few months, Garfield's owners put the latest collection in a bag to return with apologies to the rightful owners.

Jenny Reid
Otaika, Whangarei
New Zealand

115

A cat with a collecting habit

Smokey Jo and her sister Skibo were left behind when their owners moved away. Skibo was already pregnant, Smokey Jo had an untreated broken leg, and both were malnourished and infested with fleas. They coped by themselves for a while, then adopted us and moved into our house. Our existing cats, Mitsi and Mungo, happily accepted their new companions.

Smokey Jo shows her gratitude for being given a second chance by bringing us small gifts. We've been told this is a sign that she is happy.

A loud meow announces the arrival of each gift. Early one morning she brought us a beautiful piece of steak. Presumably somebody had left it out in their kitchen overnight to defrost. About a week later, she came home dragging a string of sausages behind her. She is quite a small black cat, so she looked like something out of a 'Tom and Jerry' cartoon.

That afternoon she returned with a freshly baked sausage roll. I imagine that whoever had left the sausages out overnight had now done their baking. We have apologised to various neighbours but have never discovered whose kitchen she raids.

There is, however, a strange sort of logic to Smokey Jo's gifts. If my mother comes to stay for the weekend she spends most of her time reading the newspaper, and by Sunday the living room is carpeted with discarded papers. This obviously registers with Smokey Jo, who deduces that we must want lots of old newspapers. She will spend the next week dragging various tatty bits of newspaper through the cat flap and into the house.

If we leave clothes drying on radiators or piles of clothes waiting to be ironed, this also registers with Smokey Jo. We clearly want more clothes. She'll spend the next few days bringing the neighbours' clothes back to the house. She's particularly partial to baby clothes and baseball caps. Gloves – both gardening and goalkeeping – are other favourites. Sometimes we find that our own socks and underwear have been moved around the house, and we worry that perhaps she has taken a pair of our knickers as a gift to a favoured neighbour.

On a workday morning when the alarm goes off, I grab my watch and go downstairs. At the weekend, if Smokey Jo decides that we are sleeping in too long, she'll pick up the watch in her mouth and throw it at us. It's her way of telling us to get up and get her breakfast.

Each week when the bin men collect the rubbish, they leave a plastic bin liner for each house. Smokey Jo sees us collect ours, then goes round all the rest of the street's front gardens, collects theirs and brings them home for us. It is slightly embarrassing that we have a never-ending supply whereas the neighbours have to buy theirs from the shops. Presumably it's Smokey Jo's way of contributing to the housekeeping.

You are warned to keep your pets in on Guy Fawkes night so they're not scared by the fireworks. Smokey Jo must be the only pet that does the warning herself.

Flyers advertising a local fireworks display had been stuck in people's letter boxes. Smokey Jo saw that we had one so decided we must want some more. She pulled all the flyers out of the letter boxes in the street and brought them home to us. Needless to say, our cats were safely locked indoors on November 5.

One evening, Smokey Jo jumped on the table while we were having dinner. She knocked over a drink and we told her off. She was clearly upset, as the following morning when we came downstairs we found she had taken everything movable out of our greenhouse and deposited the items in our kitchen. The kitchen floor was covered in seed packets, plant ties, gloves, plant name tags and so on. She must have been going backwards and forwards, carrying things, all night.

117

We tried to stop her night-time forays by locking her in at night but she soon learned how to open the cat flap, even when it was locked, and continued her patrols.

When Skibo gave birth to five kittens, Smokey Jo was the perfect auntie. She took on babysitting duties and happily played with her nephews and nieces for hours. When the kittens were rehomed she seemed to miss them even more than Skibo, their mother.

Helen and Neil Munro
Stonehouse, Gloucestershire
England

Now, how can I get my chair back?

Years ago I lived in a small village in southern France. I came home one day to find a thin black and white cat with half a tail wandering around. I invited him in for a drink of milk and he stayed for the rest of his life.

Wuss, as he came to be known, spent most of his time in the kitchen. It was the warmest room in the old stone house and he had his chair, with a cushion on it, right beside the stove. In hot weather he would sit half in, half out of the open window, enjoying the cool draught.

One day I had just washed my hair and sat down on the cat's chair by the stove to get it dry. Wuss was eating his meal on the other side of the room.

When he had finished he ambled over to his usual seat, found it occupied and stared up at me. I invited him onto my lap but that was *not* what he wanted. He stood there, apparently deep in thought, then walked to the door. I got up to let him out … and he promptly doubled back and jumped onto his chair. I decided that he deserved to stay there.

Heather Willings
Motcombe, Shaftesbury, Dorset
England

Write to me … ✉
Email Heather
h.willings@btinternet.com

Wuss was determined to have the chair

Minha contributed to the housekeeping

I adopted Minha from the local shelter. She made herself at home with my Border collie and me, and presented us with three kittens.

That was when the problems began. As soon as she felt the kittens were old enough to be left – or possibly that the dog and I could be trusted with them – she took to disappearing for a couple of hours

119

every afternoon. That in itself was no problem; it was what she came home with that was worrying.

The first time it was a bag of very fresh mince, obviously straight from the butcher's. The bag hadn't even been opened. I couldn't imagine where she could have found it; maybe someone had dropped it on their way past our house.

The next day she appeared with a bag containing fresh fish. Again it was unopened. There followed more fish, still bagged, and some cooked chicken which looked as though it had just emerged from the oven. I stood in the garden and listened to see if I could hear anyone shouting. I was sure no one would have given her the food, as people around were not known for being fond of cats.

All was quiet for a couple of days, and then she appeared with another bag of fresh fish. Had she taken it from someone's kitchen, or perhaps stolen it from a passing shopping basket? I began to dread going out, for fear that someone would stop me and demand recompense.

Her last triumph was a large bag of mince. She'd dragged it along the front path from the main road. I was amazed that she'd managed to get it home at all. She called out to me and her family to show off what she had brought, and perhaps to get help taking it inside.

I never did find out where Minha found her treasures. I made a few discreet enquiries but no one seemed to know about any strange disappearances of food.

I have a feeling that she was doing her best to help supplement the diet of her three kittens. It was her way of contributing to the housekeeping.

Hazel Tipping
Wickford, Essex
England

Only Minha will ever know where all her 'acquisitions' came from

How did the cat know my shoe size?

Ruairi is an Havana, a member of the Siamese cat family. He came into our lives when he was 12 weeks old, and not only did he have character, he had an attitude problem.

Six foot fences had almost always ensured that our previous Siamese, Teddy, stayed in our large back garden. Not so with Ruairi. It was quite funny to see this tiny green-eyed brown kitten run up the fence and onto the garage belonging to our next-door neighbours, Janet and Doug. He would march down their path and enter their conservatory through the cat flap, where he was in territory belonging to Sammy, their fluffy white kitten. Ruairi and Sammy roamed the neighbourhood together.

When Ruairi developed his hunting instinct, wildlife was unfortunately thin on the ground in the built-up area where we lived. He started to bring home Sammy's toys instead. We simply threw them back over the fence. Then soft toys started to appear.

We asked Janet if they were hers but they weren't. My husband Colin and I checked with various neighbours but had no luck. The collection was growing so we asked the local priest if they were perhaps being collected for a garden fete or something of the sort. No. One day Ruairi brought home an enormous fluffy hedgehog; goodness knows how he got it over the six foot fence.

About a week later, Doug knocked at the door to ask if we had a hedgehog. Janet had bought it as a present for a friend's toddler. She'd put it on a high shelf but, when she went to retrieve it, it was gone. How Ruairi had got it through the cat flap in their kitchen door and then through the one in their conservatory defies imagination.

He was always an early morning thief, and one morning he brought us a brand new turquoise sheepskin moccasin. I assumed it was Janet's and threw it over the back fence. Next day he brought it back again. This time I put it through Janet's letter box so she would

Ruairi with his stolen slippers

see it as she left for work. Ruairi brought it back again the following day.

That evening, when I heard Janet in her garden, I hopped up on a garden bench to call to her over the fence. 'I knew that slipper must have something to do with Ruairi,' she said, laughing.

'I've only just noticed that the size on the bottom is eight, and I'll bet you only take a four,' I replied. The slipper hung around in our conservatory, and one day when Ruairi was being a nuisance I said,

123

'Why don't you go and get the other slipper, then I'll have a pair?'

Believe it or not, the very next morning Ruairi brought me the other slipper. And I actually take size eight.

When we moved to Ireland I decided there was no way that Ruairi was taking all his loot with him. In any case, he has plenty of soft toys of his own. We let him keep the pink panther and a white cat, and I kept the slippers.

Stephanie Handley
Dungloe, County Donegal
Ireland

9

Smart cats touch our hearts

Bell reminds me to chase the butterflies

I had voluntarily cleaned Annabelle's pen one day a week. She had been there for four years and no one had chosen her as their own cat.

I'd call her name and she'd come running for hugs and treats: a little extra brushing, some salve on a hurt, a face washing. When I moved to cleaning the kitten pen, I tried to end my time with Annabelle. Only, now I knew that she was a 'he'. Somehow I had missed that detail when I named the marmalade and white cat.

Along came kitten season and, with one thing and another, I hadn't seen Annabelle for a bit so was shocked to find him languishing in a cage reserved for the very sick. Always skinny, his bones appeared to protrude through his skin. Curled in a ball in his litter, he was encrusted with his own filth and his nose was plugged with gunk.

My heart caught in my throat: Annabelle had given up. Ignoring the 'you can't save them all', 'you have too many' mantras, I took him home and placed him in a cage on my porch. A long nap refreshed him enough to worry about his grooming and to enquire about the menu.

These days, several daily walkabouts give him plenty of opportunities to tiptoe along the edge of the sidewalk straight to a favourite tree to hone claws and stretch tall, check the birdbath and then the feeders for lingerers, peek in the woods, taste a few weeds,

125

inspect the hiding places under the canoe, trot to the end of the driveway to look this way and that, hide in the shade among the impatiens to watch the grass grow and the ladybugs do their work, seek a lap or a shoulder for a nap, tell the neighbour's cat to go home, and chase noisy squirrels up a tree. This accomplished, he can return to his pen to lie before the fan and listen to classical music while slurping some Nutrical (a dietary supplement). Bell has earned his time in the sun.

What life will hold for Bell is as much a mystery as it is for each of us. For now, we'll take it one hug at a time. And, when it's my turn to be up against it, I want to remember a scrawny, sickly, sneezing, coughing cat dancing after a yellow butterfly flitting over the freshly mowed lawn. Annabelle, you go ~~girl~~ boy.

Madelyn Filipski
Cape May County, New Jersey
United States

Mamma-cat was afraid of nothing

I was naive enough to think that most cats were like her. We didn't even bother to give her a proper name, calling her only 'the mamma-cat'.

For most of my young life, she was the only cat I knew. She was a domestic shorthair, I guess; her coat was often dusty but when it was clean it was a subdued tortoiseshell-tabby. I think she was at least 13. She was a good mother, raising at least one litter each year. Some of them she delivered on my bed while I was still sleeping in it. She hunted constantly and I would see her carrying a mouse or gopher to the kittens in summer. She wasn't above getting up on the kitchen

126

Bell didn't let his tough start in life get him down

counter and helping herself whenever she could. But she didn't really need us at all, and she came to the house only when she chose.

Mamma-cat was by far the most intelligent cat I've seen. She could let herself into the house by jumping up on the railing and putting her paws on top of the doorknob. I watched her do this several times, and she made it look very easy.

Fiercely protective, Mamma-cat once mauled our German shepherd King when he took offence at our Siamese Bitsy being too close to his food. Bitsy was expecting kittens and both cats tore into him like dervishes. When it was all over I was amazed that, aside from being a little shaken, Bitsy was relatively intact and delivered a healthy litter soon after. King, however, was covered in scratches and bites, including a baffling number on his tongue. Mamma-cat didn't even come close to being hurt.

I followed her, watching her hunting style. She was more patient than I could ever be. I tried to emulate her, lying down next to the gopher holes and watching the baby gophers at play. They would come so close that I could have caught them with my bare hands.

I didn't realise just how powerful and graceful a cat could be until I witnessed another of her hunting activities. My brothers and I were chasing pigeons out of the loft of the barn and Mamma-cat was following us, as she often did. The last pigeon was flying towards the vent window in the gable end of the barn. Mamma-cat jumped up, *away* from the pigeon, against the side of a vertical timber, for the split second it took to bounce up and off it, and, twisting in the air, caught the pigeon on the wing. I was amazed. She made it look so easy that I can only imagine she did it often.

I believe she showed a level of complex thought and physical coordination that few humans could achieve. Merely shooting a clay pigeon out of the air with a shotgun took me years to accomplish, and I'm not very good at it. When it came to evaluating her environment and determining which action would result in a favourable outcome, she was far more capable than most people are. Perhaps it was for the best that we never got around to naming her. I don't think we could have picked a name that would do her personality justice.

I found Mamma-cat dead one day. I don't know what had finally gotten her. There was nothing she was afraid of, or incapable of handling. I suspect it was old age. She was on her favourite hunting grounds, and so I left her there.

T R Hayward
Virden, Manitoba
Canada

Tabby Tiger turned my life around

Tabby Tiger entered my kitchen and my life at a time when I had almost lost my self-esteem, my career and my health. Although I did not recognise it immediately, he was the impetus I needed to turn my world around.

I was on long-term sickness absence and hadn't been responding to medication for fibromyalgia and severe depression. I seemed to be drowning in a terrible rut where even the basics were becoming unmanageable.

On this particular day in April I had left my kitchen door slightly ajar. From the corner of my eye I could see movement near the back door. I peered around the door and thought I saw a tail disappear past the corner of my house. At long last an emotion stirred inside me.

I found some dry cat food in my cupboard; it had been left over from when I had looked after the cat Thomas next door. I hurriedly

threw some kibbles on a saucer near the corner, returned to the kitchen and waited with baited breath. My patience was rewarded when I watched a frightened but starving cat venture timidly around the corner, checking the whole time that the coast was clear. It proceeded to devour the contents of the saucer.

Quietly I made myself known and spoke softly while I offered more food. He retreated behind the corner again but I knew he was watching me refill the saucer. He cleared the plate once more and I repeated the procedure four or five times. On the last occasion, I pulled the door open as far as it would go and retreated to my dining room, carefully watching the kitchen. Again my patience was rewarded as he timidly entered, sniffing the air and checking that he was safe.

I lost track of the time, and in any case it was of no importance to me. I maintained my distance and watched the little explorer find his way, eventually, to my bedroom and the warmth of my feather duvet. I gave him time to settle and then left him alone to rest, returning throughout the day to make sure he was okay. Eventually I could get close enough to see whether he wore a collar so that I could trace his possible owner, and examine him for any injuries. He smelled like a drain, with bloated tummy and ticks gorging themselves on his ears, sure signs that he'd been living rough for some time.

The hardest thing for me to do – with my depression – was to make an appointment with a vet and leave the safety of my home to go shopping for cat food and other sundries. But, apart from a sizeable tapeworm, Tabby Tiger turned out to be in reasonable health. And, amazingly, my depression was at long last beginning to lift.

At first it was imperceptible, but after two years of caring for Tabby Tiger I was finally weaned off antidepressants. Fibromyalgia is a form of arthritis. Treatment is only palliative and the disease is progressive. Tabby Tiger came into his own when I had an arthritic flare-up. He seems to know when I am at my worst, and when I have to take to my bed he's there to keep me company. He makes no demands at these times, as if he knows that my condition will eventually ease off and we can return to our usual routine.

He will put himself between me and an unfamiliar visitor to protect me, and when I'm in the kitchen he will make his presence known by calling out so that I don't trip over him. Tabby Tiger has been my constant companion and carer for the past seven years. He now has medication for heart disease but, despite his own problems, he is always there for me.

In 2003 he was a runner-up in the Best Friends category of the Cats Protection Rescue Cat of the Year award, and in 2004 he was

Tabby Tiger with his Britain's Top Cat award

131

voted Britain's Top Cat in the Kitzyme Cat of the Year award. More recently, a magazine nominated him for a Creature of Companionship award.

I am indebted to him for turning my life around. Despite the fact that I am now medically retired, I couldn't be happier.

Theresa M Carrier
Northwich, Cheshire
England

He chose to spend his last night on my settee

'Oh no, it's not one of mine, it's one I found on the settee this morning.' These were the words I uttered in response to the question I had just been asked. The murmuring of other people in the room instantly stopped, and heads swivelled to stare at me. I'd been telling them about taking a cat to the vet.

I had come downstairs as usual that morning, to appease the hunger pangs of the three felines who condescended to live with me. I glanced around the room, and on the settee lay a strange tabby cat, watching me intently, as if to assess my reaction.

I walked over to him but he made no effort to move. I lifted him gently onto the floor, where he promptly collapsed. I stood him up again but to my dismay he collapsed immediately.

I decided to take him to the vet and placed him on a blanket in a box. Telling my cats I would feed them something special when I returned, I drove to the vet. The receptionist asked which of my cats needed attention, and I explained about finding a stranger on the settee. The vet examined the poor creature, and told me that he was an elderly 'street' tomcat and that, sadly, all his organs had ceased to function. The kindest thing to do was euthanise the cat. Did I want to stay with him? I couldn't face that and, to my horror, I burst into tears. I drove home in a very sombre mood, to be reassured by the presence of my three hungry moggies.

How the tabby cat had managed to climb through the cat flap and then onto the settee I will never know, but both the vet and I were pleased that his final night had been a comfortable one, although I'd hoped for a happier outcome.

Mrs Stella Palmer
Sheffield
England

The matriarch

A large grassy bank snaked its way along the boundary of our house, and a cinder lane separated our property from a small row of terraced houses. By some architectural feat, a concrete coal bunker had been built within the body of the bank, giving the impression that this man-made creation was one with nature. We had our first sighting of the matriarch on the top of that coal bunker.

As the resident trainee cat expert, I was called upon by Mother to view the creature from the safety of a small side window in our kitchen. She was a smallish black cat, huddled into a corner where the bank broke away from the bunker, an air of desolation about her.

This was a cat who had been a victim of life in a harsh West Cumbrian village where cats were seen as vermin, often poisoned or stolen by someone who purportedly killed them and sold the fur. She had obviously been mated with every tomcat in the village, for her ears were ripped to shreds and had healed into distorted shapes. Her lower jaw was either badly broken or had been dislocated.

133

Tiger and Blackie (fully grown) – the last of Tattyhead's kittens

I found an old feeding bowl, forked out some of my Siamese cat's bounty, slowly opened the back door and made my way to the bunker. I had a healthy respect for cats, particularly the lightning speed of fangs and claws. She ate with gusto; mother nature had given her a break, after all. One of us named her Tattyhead and that's who she became to us: a lonely feral cat who was not for taming but surprisingly found it in her heart to purr when she was given food and drink. She disappeared as silently as she had arrived. Her life was in stark contrast to the comfortable life Zemoy shared with us and we decided to keep them absolutely separate.

Over the next few months Tattyhead reappeared now and again, until mealtimes on the bunker became a regular part of our routine. Eventually she must have decided to share her good fortune with her family. At first she came with her black male partner, and we recognised him as Jo Sharp's cat. Jo was a quiet widower who lived in

134

one of the terraced houses on the other side of our cinder lane, and, not knowing his cat's name, we called him Mr Tattyhead, although he was in relatively good condition.

Then came the kittens. Over the summer months there would be a new addition to the Tattyhead clan, each more handsome than the last. Mr and Mrs Tattyhead presented their offspring on the coal bunker lid each time, until there were as many as 11, each vying for food but knowing their place in the pecking order. Was it our imagination, or was each generation becoming less afraid of us? As they grew up they disappeared in turn, until the last pair of twins – one black and the other a beautifully marked brown tabby – was presented for inspection.

It transpired one day that Tattyhead died doing what she did best – producing kittens. She was last seen struggling to walk, with the arm of a dead kitten protruding from her cervix. Before anyone could reach her and seek medical attention, she melted back into the bank, as mysteriously as she had arrived.

Theresa M Carrier
Northwich, Cheshire
England

We both needed a friend

It was a gorgeous summer evening in late January 2002, and I was sitting at my table facing the ranchslider out to the deck.

I looked up and there he was, staring back at me. A tiny, skinny, pathetic-looking cat. Our eyes met and he was gone. I went outside for a closer inspection and he ran to me, purring. His emaciated little body was bald, the fleas and ticks were having a right royal time on him and his bones stuck out. He was covered in dirt and

135

had obviously not groomed himself for some time. But his face was untouched, jet black with beautiful golden eyes. From the moment I saw him, I knew I wanted to adopt him. I named him Bailey.

The next day, a freak accident put me in hospital with a badly broken ankle. Thanks to my wonderful local vets, who looked after him until I could, I was able to keep Bailey and he became my constant companion while I was recuperating. He was a sweetheart, with a most delightful personality, and I really loved him.

However, I became concerned that he wasn't putting much weight on, even though all his fur grew back. Following a blood test, I received devastating news: my Bailey had contracted the feline aids (FIV) virus when he was living rough. There was no cure, and I didn't know how much longer he would live.

One day when I came home from work, Bailey was unwell and sitting on my bed. He turned and stared at me with a look I will never forget. I took him to the vet, who confirmed my fears that there was no more they could do. The next day the vet came to my home and Bailey passed away peacefully in my arms.

The odd thing is, no one had ever seen this cat before. My neighbours hadn't seen him hanging around; it was as if he'd dropped from the sky. And I'd noticed that while I was incapacitated his health was great, but as I got stronger and returned to work his health deteriorated. I've often wondered if he somehow knew an accident was about to befall me and realised I would need a friend, and that he knew he didn't have long to go and needed a friend too. I know I'll never forget him.

Mary O'Sullivan
Paraparaumu
New Zealand

Guardian angel

People say that everyone has an angel watching over them, and that they come into our lives when we need them most.

There's no telling what form an angel could take. Mine appeared one autumn afternoon – thin, grey and pressing a cold nose to my patio door. I've always had a soft spot for waifs and strays, and strangers will be offered a good meal and made welcome in my home, so in he came.

He looked as though he'd travelled far, for his coat was dirty and a little thin in places. I served him up a dish of tuna and asked his name and where he came from, but he declined to answer. After dinner we sat in the lounge in front of the fire, the television on in the background, and again I spoke to my guest. 'What brings you here?' I asked. 'Will anyone be wondering where you are?' But he wasn't in a very talkative mood. In fact, my guest fell asleep curled tightly on my lap, so I decided I would do the talking.

I told him what had happened to me that day. The man I loved had left with a suitcase of clothes, and I knew he wouldn't be back. I had known for a long time that this was going to happen, and for a long time I had been sad.

That night, for the first time, I cried. I wept for the man I had once loved and had now lost, I wept because I was scared of being alone. My tears rolled down my cheeks and some dripped onto my guest's grey coat. They stuck to it like little pearls, and as I stroked him he became damp, for which I apologised.

The next morning after breakfast I opened the door and stepped outside. It was a nice day, the air was clear, and as the clouds parted I was bathed in warm golden sunshine from head to toe. When I opened my eyes again, he was sitting at my feet.

I touched his head and said, 'Everything's going to be okay.' He jumped onto the fence and paused for a few seconds, giving me a look that seemed to say, *You don't need me here any more*. Then he was gone.

That day I felt free. In fact, I felt happier than I had done for a long time. When evening came, I found myself looking at the patio door just to see if by any chance he was there. But as I turned out the light I knew our paths had crossed that night only because we had both needed them to. As I drew the curtains, I whispered, 'Thank you' for the unexpected guest who had listened, comforted and reassured when I needed it most. A real guardian angel.

Katharine Greene
Ramsgate, Kent
England

The SMARTER than JACK story

We hope you've enjoyed this book. The SMARTER than JACK books are exciting and entertaining to create and so far we've raised over NZ$280,000 to help animals. We are thrilled!

Here's my story about how the SMARTER than JACK series came about.

Until late 1999 my life was a seemingly endless search for the elusive 'fulfilment'. I had this feeling that I was put on this earth to make a difference, but I had no idea how. Coupled with this, I had low self-confidence – not a good combination! This all left me feeling rather frustrated, lonely and unhappy with life. I'd always had a creative streak and loved animals. In my early years I spent many hours designing things such as horse saddles, covers and cat and dog beds. I even did a stint as a professional pet photographer.

Then I remembered something I was once told: do something for the right reasons and good things will come. So that's what I did. I set about starting Avocado Press and creating the first New Zealand edition in the SMARTER than JACK series. It was released in 2002 and all the profit went to the Royal New Zealand SPCA.

Good things did come. People were thrilled to be a part of the book and many were first-time writers. Readers were enthralled and many were delighted to receive the book as a gift from friends and family. The Royal New Zealand SPCA was over $43,000 better off and I received many encouraging letters and emails from readers and contributors. What could be better than that?

How could I stop there! It was as if I had created a living thing with the SMARTER than JACK series; it seemed to have a life all of its own. I now had the responsibility of evolving it. It had to continue to benefit animals and people by providing entertainment, warmth and something that people could feel part of. What an awesome responsibility and opportunity, albeit a bit of a scary one!

It is my vision to make SMARTER than JACK synonymous with smart animals, and a household name all over the world. The concept is already becoming well known as a unique and effective way for animal welfare charities to raise money, to encourage additional donors and to instil a greater respect for animals. The series is now in Australia, New Zealand, the United States, Canada and the United Kingdom.

Avocado Press, as you may have guessed, is a little different. We are about more than just creating books; we're about sharing information and experiences, and developing things in innovative ways. Ideas are most welcome too.

We feel it's possible to run a successful business that is both profitable and that contributes to animal welfare in a significant way. We want people to enjoy and talk about our books; that way, ideas are shared and the better it becomes for everyone.

Thank you for reading my story.

Jenny Campbell
Creator of SMARTER than JACK

Submit a story for our books

We are always creating more exciting books in the SMARTER than JACK series. Your true stories are continually being sought.

You can have a look at our website www.smarterthanjack.com. Here you can read stories, find information on how to submit stories, and read entertaining and interesting animal news. You can also sign up to receive the Story of the Week by email. We'd love to hear your ideas, too, on how to make the next books even better.

Guidelines for stories

- The story must be true and about a smart animal or animals.
- The story should be about 100 to 1000 words in length. We may edit it and you will be sent a copy to approve prior to publication.
- The story must be written from your point of view, not the animal's.
- Photographs and illustrations are welcome if they enhance the story, and if used will most likely appear in black and white.
- Submissions can be sent by post to SMARTER than JACK (see addresses on the following page) or via the website at www.smarterthanjack.com
- Include your name, postal and email address, and phone number, and indicate if you do not wish your name to be included with your story.
- Handwritten submissions are perfectly acceptable, but if you can type them, so much the better.
- Posted submissions will not be returned unless a stamped self-addressed envelope is provided.
- The writers of stories selected for publication will be notified prior to publication.
- Stories are welcome from everybody, and given the charitable nature of our projects there will be no prize money awarded, just recognition for successful submissions.

- Particpating animal welfare charities and Avocado Press have the right to publish extracts from the stories received without restriction of location or publication, provided the publication of those extracts helps promote the SMARTER than JACK series.

Where to send your story

Online
- Use the submission form at www.smarterthanjack.com or email it to submissions@smarterthanjack.com.

By post
- **In Australia**
  PO Box 170, Ferntree Gully, VIC 3156, Australia
- **In Canada and the United States**
  PO Box 819, Tottenham, ON, L0G 1W0, Canada
- **In New Zealand and rest of world**
  PO Box 27003, Wellington, New Zealand

Receive a free
SMARTER than JACK gift pack

Did you know that around half our customers buy the SMARTER than JACK books as gifts? We appreciate this and would like to thank and reward those who do so. If you buy eight books in the SMARTER than JACK series we will send you a free gift pack.

All you need to do is buy your eight books and either attach the receipt for each book or, if you ordered by mail, just write the date that you placed the order in one of the spaces on the next page. Then complete your details on the form, cut out the page and post it to us. We will then send you your SMARTER than JACK gift pack. Feel free to photocopy this form – that will save cutting a page out of the book.

Do you have a dog or a cat? You can choose from either a cat or dog gift pack. Just indicate your preference.

Note that the contents of the SMARTER than JACK gift pack will vary from country to country, but may include:
- The SMARTER than JACK mini Collector Series
- SMARTER than JACK postcards
- Soft animal toy
- Books in the SMARTER than JACK series

Show your purchases here:

Book 1	Book 2	Book 3	Book 4
Receipt attached ☐ *or* Date ordered _____	Receipt attached ☐ *or* Date ordered _____	Receipt attached ☐ *or* Date ordered _____	Receipt attached ☐ *or* Date ordered _____
Book 5	Book 6	Book 7	Book 8
Receipt attached ☐ *or* Date ordered _____	Receipt attached ☐ *or* Date ordered _____	Receipt attached ☐ *or* Date ordered _____	Receipt attached ☐ *or* Date ordered _____

Complete your details:

Your name: _____

Street address: _____

City/town: _____

State: _____

Postcode: _____

Country: _____

Phone: _____

Email: _____

Would you like a cat or dog gift pack?   CAT/DOG

Post the completed page to us:

- **In Australia**
  PO Box 170, Ferntree Gully, VIC 3156, Australia
- **In Canada and the United States**
  PO Box 819, Tottenham, ON, L0G 1W0, Canada
- **In New Zealand and rest of world**
  PO Box 27003, Wellington, New Zealand

Please allow four weeks for delivery.

Get more wonderful stories

Now you can receive a fantastic new-release SMARTER than JACK book every three months. That's a new book every March, June, September and December. The books are delivered to your door. It's easy!

Here's a sample of what you'd get if you signed up for four books over one year (option 2 on the order form) in September 2005:

- *Cats are SMARTER than JACK* in September 2005
- *Dogs are SMARTER than JACK* in December 2005
- *Heroic animals are SMARTER than JACK* in March 2006
- *Cheeky animals are SMARTER than JACK* in June 2006

Every time you get a book you will also receive a copy of *Smart Animals*, our members-only newsletter. Postage is included in the subscription price if the delivery address is in the United States, Canada, the United Kingdom, Australia or New Zealand.

You can also purchase existing titles in the SMARTER than JACK series. To purchase a book you can either go to your local bookstore or participating animal welfare charity, or order using the form at the end of the book.

How your purchase will help animals

The amount our partner animal welfare charities receive varies according to how the books are sold and the country in which they are sold. Contact your local participating animal welfare charity for more information.

In Australia

Smarter than Jack Limited is accepting orders on behalf of the RSPCA in Australia. Please send your order to:

SMARTER than JACK, PO Box 170, Ferntree Gully, VIC 3156

In Canada

The Canadian Federation of Humane Societies is accepting orders on behalf of the participating animal welfare charities in Canada, as listed below. Please send your order to:

CFHS, 102-30 Concourse Gate, Ottawa, ON, K2E 7V7

Please nominate from the following list the participating animal welfare charity that you would like to benefit from your book purchase:

- Alberta SPCA
- Bide A While Animal Shelter Society
- Calgary Humane Society
- Cochrane Humane Society
- Hamilton/Burlington SPCA
- Lakeland Humane Society
- Mae Bachur Animal Shelter
- Meadowlake and District Humane Society
- Newfoundland & Labrador SPCA
- Nova Scotia Humane Society
- Ontario SPCA
- Ottawa Humane Society
- PEI Humane Society
- Red Deer and District SPCA
- Saskatchewan SPCA
- SPA de l'Estrie
- Winnipeg Humane Society

In New Zealand

Please send your order to:

Royal New Zealand SPCA National Office, PO Box 15349, New Lynn, Auckland 1232

In the United Kingdom

Smarter than Jack Limited is accepting orders on behalf of the participating animal welfare charities in the United Kingdom, as listed below. Please send your order to:

SMARTER than JACK, FREEPOST NAT 11465, Northampton, NN3 6BR

Please nominate from the following list the participating animal welfare charity that you would like to benefit from your book purchase:

- Cats Protection
- Dogs Trust

In the United States

Smarter than Jack Limited is accepting orders on behalf of the participating animal welfare charities in the United States, as listed below. Please send your order to:

SMARTER than JACK, 45 High Street N, Thunder Bay, ON, P7A 5R1, CANADA

Please nominate from the following list the participating animal welfare charity that you would like to benefit from your book purchase:

- Alley Cat Allies
- American Humane Association
- Animal Rescue Foundation Inc.
- Cat Care Society
- Feral Friends Animal Rescue and Assistance
- Humane Society of Lewisville
- Jeff Davis County Humane Society
- People for the Ethical Treatment of Animals (PETA)
- Pets911
- West Plains Regional Animal Shelter

Rest of world

Please send your order to:
SMARTER than JACK, PO Box 27003, Wellington,
NEW ZEALAND

Purchase from your local bookstore

Your local bookstore should have the editions you want or, if not, be able to order them for you. If they can't get the books, the publisher Avocado Press can be contacted direct:
By email: orders@smarterthanjack.com
By post: Avocado Press Limited, PO Box 27003, Wellington,
NEW ZEALAND

Order online

To order online go to www.supportanimals.com

How much are the books?

- Australia $19.95
- Canada $17.95 plus taxes
- New Zealand $19.95
- United Kingdom £7.99
- United States $11.95 plus taxes

Order form

What books would you like?

A new-release book every three months

The books are sent out in March, June, September and December. You will receive your first book in the appropriate month after we receive your order.

	Quantity	Total
Option 1: two books over six months	2	
Option 2: four books over one year	4	
Option 3: eight books over two years	8	
Existing books in the series		
Animals are SMARTER than JACK (2005) *Canada and the USA only*		
Cats are SMARTER than JACK (2005)		
Dogs are SMARTER than JACK (2005)		
Australian animals are SMARTER than JACK 1 (2003) *Australia only*		
Australian animals are SMARTER than JACK 2 (2004) *Australia only*		
Canadian animals are SMARTER than JACK 1 (2004) *Canada only*		
Why animals are SMARTER than US (2004) *Australia, New Zealand, Canada and the USA only*		
Applicable taxes		
Subtotal for order		
Packaging and post: for orders of existing books only, please add $5 or £2		
Total		

For Canada, United States and United Kingdom orders only – using the lists on the preceding pages, please indicate which animal welfare charity in your country you would like to benefit from your order:

Choose the payment method

There are two ways you can pay:

- By cheque/check/postal order made out to the organisation you are sending it to and posted, along with your completed order form, to one of the addresses listed or
- Fill in the credit card details below:

Card type: Visa/Mastercard

Card number: ⬚⬚⬚⬚⬚⬚⬚⬚⬚⬚⬚⬚⬚⬚⬚⬚⬚⬚⬚

Name on card: _____   Expiry date: _____

Complete your details

Your name: _____
Street address: _____
City/town: _____
State: _____
Postcode: _____
Country: _____
Phone: _____
Email: _____

Send in your order

Post your order to your nearest participating animal welfare charity or Smarter than Jack Limited at one of the addresses listed on pages 146–148, according to which country you live in.

Please note that some of the books are only available in certain countries.